Current
CONTROVERSIES

Pollution

Other books in the Current Controversies series

Pollution

Debra A. Miller, Book Editor

GREENHAVEN PRESS

An imprint of Thomson Gale, a part of The Thomson Corporation

Detroit • New York • San Francisco • New Haven, Conn. • Waterville, Maine • London

Christine Nasso, *Publisher*
Elizabeth Des Chenes, *Managing Editor*

© 2007 Thomson Gale, a part of The Thomson Corporation.

Thomson and Star logo are trademarks and Gale and Greenhaven Press are registered trademarks used herein under license.

For more information, contact:
Greenhaven Press
27500 Drake Rd.
Farmington Hills, MI 48331-3535
Or you can visit our Internet site at http://www.gale.com

LIBRARY OF CONGRESS CATALOGING-IN-PUBLICATION DATA

Pollution / Debra A. Miller, Editor.
    p. cm. -- (Current controversies)
  Includes bibliographical references and index.
  ISBN-13: 978-0-7377-3727-1 (hardcover)
  ISBN-13: 978-0-7377-3728-8 (pbk.)
  1. Air pollution. 2. Water pollution. I. Miller, Debra A.
  TD883.P58 2007
  363.73--dc22

                                        2007017972

ISBN-10: 0-7377-3727-1 (hardcover)
ISBN-10: 0-7377-3728-X (pbk.)

Printed in the United States of America
10 9 8 7 6 5 4 3 2 1

Contents

Chapter 2: Are Corporations Polluting the Environment?

Chapter 3: Are U.S. Pollution Regulations Effective?

Foreword

By definition, controversies are "discussions of questions in which opposing opinions clash" (Webster's Twentieth Century Dictionary Unabridged). Few would deny that controversies are a pervasive part of the human condition and exist on virtually every level of human enterprise. Controversies transpire between individuals and among groups, within nations and between nations. Controversies supply the grist necessary for progress by providing challenges and challengers to the status quo. They also create atmospheres where strife and warfare can flourish. A world without controversies would be a peaceful world; but it also would be, by and large, static and prosaic.

The Series' Purpose

The purpose of the Current Controversies series is to explore many of the social, political, and economic controversies dominating the national and international scenes today. Titles selected for inclusion in the series are highly focused and specific. For example, from the larger category of criminal justice, Current Controversies deals with specific topics such as police brutality, gun control, white collar crime, and others. The debates in Current Controversies also are presented in a useful, timeless fashion. Articles and book excerpts included in each title are selected if they contribute valuable, long-range ideas to the overall debate. And wherever possible, current information is enhanced with historical documents and other relevant materials. Thus, while individual titles are current in focus, every effort is made to ensure that they will not become quickly outdated. Books in the Current Controversies series will remain important resources for librarians, teachers, and students for many years.

In addition to keeping the titles focused and specific, great care is taken in the editorial format of each book in the series. Book introductions and chapter prefaces are offered to provide background material for readers. Chapters are organized around several key questions that are answered with diverse opinions representing all points on the political spectrum. Materials in each chapter include opinions in which authors clearly disagree as well as alternative opinions in which authors may agree on a broader issue but disagree on the possible solutions. In this way, the content of each volume in Current Controversies mirrors the mosaic of opinions encountered in society. Readers will quickly realize that there are many viable answers to these complex issues. By questioning each author's conclusions, students and casual readers can begin to develop the critical thinking skills so important to evaluating opinionated material.

Current Controversies is also ideal for controlled research. Each anthology in the series is composed of primary sources taken from a wide gamut of informational categories including periodicals, newspapers, books, U. S. and foreign government documents, and the publications of private and public organizations. Readers will find factual support for reports, debates, and research papers covering all areas of important issues. In addition, an annotated table of contents, an index, a book and periodical bibliography, and a list of organizations to contact are included in each book to expedite further research.

Perhaps more than ever before in history, people are confronted with diverse and contradictory information. During the Persian Gulf War, for example, the public was not only treated to minute-to-minute coverage of the war, it was also inundated with critiques of the coverage and countless analyses of the factors motivating U.S. involvement. Being able to sort through the plethora of opinions accompanying today's major issues, and to draw one's own conclusions, can be a complicated and frustrating struggle. It is the editors' hope that Current Controversies will help readers with this struggle.

Introduction

"Much of the credit for publicizing the threat of global warming must go to former vice president and 2000 presidential candidate Al Gore, who since his defeat in the presidential race has been touring the country and the world giving speeches on the issue."

During most of the latter half of the twentieth century, environmental problems such as air and water pollution presented relatively clear and understandable challenges to the U.S. public and government. A dark and smelly smog created by car and industrial pollutants hovered over Los Angeles and other cities; America's rivers, streams, and oceans became fouled by raw sewage, chemicals, and pesticides; and many wildlife species were threatened with extinction. All these visible problems inspired the U.S. Congress to pass a series of environmental laws in the 1960s and 1970s such as the Clean Air Act, Clean Water Act, and Endangered Species Act—laws that have helped to improve America's air, water, and land resources.

In the new millennium, a potentially even more alarming environmental issue is beginning to attract widespread attention. This new issue is global warming, a term that refers to rising world temperatures caused by the release of high levels of carbon dioxide and other so-called greenhouse gases from the burning of fossil fuels such as coal and oil. Much of the credit for publicizing the threat of global warming must go to former vice president and 2000 presidential candidate Al Gore, who since his defeat in the presidential race has been touring the country and the world giving speeches on the issue and presenting a slide show of compelling photos, graphs, and time lines. In 2006, Gore unveiled a documentary and book based on this presentation, both called by the same name—*An Inconvenient Truth*. The documentary, released in May, attracted large audiences and has been critically acclaimed, including winning the Academy Award for Best Documentary, Feature, in February 2007.

In the film, Gore uses humor, science, and personal stories to demonstrate that human activities that produce carbon dioxide and other pollutants are the cause of the rise in Earth's average temperatures. Warmer temperatures, Gore warns, are melting the polar ice caps and leading to rising sea levels that could soon flood major cities such as New York and New Orleans and substantially reduce the land mass of coastal states such as Florida. The film claims global warming may already be producing frightening weather, including stronger hurricanes, flooding, and torrential rains for some parts of the world, and record heat and drought in other areas. Gore points to Hurricane Katrina and Europe's 2003 heat wave as examples of the types of weather stresses humankind may face in the future. These climate changes, the film says, could in turn result in a myriad of other problems, everything from new mosquito-borne disease pandemics to the loss of animal species, such as the polar bear, which cannot adapt quickly enough to the temperature increases. In short, Gore calls global warming a "planetary emergency" and his central message is that the public and policy makers must act now to prevent what could become catastrophic disasters in the future.

Gore criticizes President George W. Bush for ignoring global warming for most of his presidency. Early in his administration, for example, Bush rejected U.S. participation in the Kyoto Protocol, an international agreement that sets mandatory targets for countries to reduce levels of greenhouse gas emissions. In 2004, the administration asked the National Academy of Sciences, a group of scientific scholars, to look into global warming, but then called for further study when the group reported back that rising temperatures are caused by human activities such as the burning of fossil fuels. In 2006, in a case before the U.S. Supreme Court brought by several states and environmental groups seeking to force the U.S. Environmental Protection Agency (EPA) to regulate greenhouse gases, the Bush administration argued that such gases are not air pollutants that must be regulated under the U.S. Clean Air Act. Gore and other critics have claimed that Bush and his supporters are too close to the oil and coal industries that cause greenhouse gases.

An Inconvenient Truth, however, has had its share of critics. Some critics deride it as too alarmist in tone, and others even question Gore's basic claim that most scientists agree that human activities are causing increases in temperatures and that global warming is a serious problem. In a July 2, 2006, article in the *Wall Street Journal*, for example, Massachusetts Institute of Technology atmospheric scientist Richard S. Lindzen argued, "The earth and its climate are dynamic; they are always changing even without any external forcing. . . . These . . . are clearly not issues over which debate is ended—at least not in terms of the actual science."

Policy makers, however, are facing increasing public pressure to act on global warming. In September 2006, the Bush administration announced a Climate Change Technology Program Strategic Plan to promote technological initiatives such as sequestering carbon dioxide before it enters the atmosphere and promoting hydrogen-powered cars. In December 2006, U.S. Department of the Interior secretary Dirk Kempthorne recommended that the polar bear be listed as "threatened" under the Endangered Species Act, a decision that environmentalists say would be an admission of global warming dangers. Many commentators thus expect the government to eventually reverse its position and begin to take stronger action on climate change.

Based on recent indications, it appears that global warming will be a major focus of environmental and pollution efforts in future decades. A number of the authors in *Current Controversies: Pollution* give their perspectives on this compelling issue. Other commentators discuss the status of other types of environmental problems, such as smog, ozone depletion, and water pollution. Reaching consensus about these pollution issues and ensuring a safe and healthy environment may be among the most critical challenges of the twenty-first century.

CHAPTER 1

Are Air and Water Pollution Serious Problems?

Chapter Preface

Economic development has brought wealth and better life-styles to many people, but historically, it has also been accompanied by damage to the environment. In fact, industrial growth is the major source of today's air and water pollution problems in the United States and other developed nations. The production of goods relies on energy, and typically that energy has come from burning fossil fuels such as coal, oil, and natural gas, all of which produce both toxic chemical by-products that pollute the air and water as well as so-called greenhouse gases that contribute to the warming of the planet. As people's incomes rise, they buy houses and cars, which also rely on fossil energy and contribute further to pollution. Cars and light trucks, in fact, are the largest source of urban air pollution in developed countries. Large-scale food production, meanwhile, often releases chemical pesticides, fertilizers, and animal wastes into the air, waterways, and groundwater.

Because Europe and the United States led the way in industrial development, they are the source of much of the world's existing environmental damage. Today, however, many poorer nations are also beginning to develop their economies, a trend that is creating a whole new wave of pollution that promises to have global ramifications. One example of this phenomenon is the People's Republic of China, a country of 1.3 billion people that since 1978 has been changing its economy from a Communist-style, state-controlled economy to a more market-oriented economy like that of the United States. The result has been a staggering increase in industrial manufacturing and the implementation of policies that have allowed foreign companies to invest and locate businesses in the country. The change has produced rapid economic growth, close to 9 percent a year. Today China's economy is the fourth largest in the world and it is expected to become the world's largest by the middle of the twenty-first century.

The by-product of this rapid growth, however, has been a huge increase in environmental pollution. Chinese factories routinely dump wastes and pollutants directly into China's waterways. According to the State Environmental Protection Administration (SEPA), China's environmental agency, 70 percent of the water in five of China's seven major river systems is now unsuitable for human contact. In addition, as more and more people move into the cities for work, urban water systems have become overwhelmed by human wastes. As a result of these pollution problems, half the country's population relies on contaminated water supplies.

Air pollution is an even bigger problem for the country. According to the World Bank, sixteen of the world's twenty most polluted cities are in China, and it is estimated that four hundred thousand Chinese die prematurely each year from respiratory diseases. One of the major reasons for this poor air quality is that China relies largely on coal energy, both for its power plants and for heating homes. In fact, China uses more coal than the United States, the European Union, and Japan combined. This use of coal produces greenhouse gases such as carbon dioxide, which may be changing China's weather; in recent years, China has experienced terrible natural disasters such as droughts and massive floods. China's burning of coal also has produced the world's highest levels of sulfur dioxide emissions and acid rain—a problem that damages aquatic life, forests, and agricultural crops. In addition, deforestation and farmland erosion cause huge sandstorms, even in Beijing, the country's capital. Despite these existing air quality problems, many newly wealthy Chinese are rapidly buying gas-guzzling cars, a trend that will doubtless produce even more air pollution.

Most experts agree that pollution in China has now reached crisis stage. Even Chinese officials are recognizing that pollution is creating huge costs for the government, measured in health bills, crop losses, disaster relief, and depletion of the country's precious natural resource. Nevertheless, the nation's vast bureaucracy, inadequate funding for SEPA, and entrenched local corruption have made environmental cleanup a difficult challenge. In the future, China is likely to take more aggressive steps to curb pollution and move toward more sustainable economic development, but this process will take time. In the meantime, the country will be the source of many more years of high-level air and water pollution.

Unfortunately, China's pollution problems are not confined to China, but will affect countries around the globe. Already, researchers in the United States have documented that dust and industrial toxins (such as lead, arsenic, and zinc) from China are landing in Hawaii and California. Many experts say that these Chinese pollutants are also trapping heat in Earth's atmosphere and helping to warm temperatures around the world. According to the June 11, 2006 *New York Times*, "The increase in global-warming gases from China's coal use will probably exceed that for all industrialized countries combined over the next 25 years." Even a slight rise in Earth's average temperatures, experts say, could lead to melting of glaciers and a rapid rise in sea levels, dramatic weather changes and natural disasters, the spread of tropical diseases, and the extinction of many animal and plant species.

China is not alone, however; other countries with large populations are also developing their economies. India, for example, has also begun to industrialize using coal-fired power plants, and its population is growing and expected to eclipse China's huge population by 2030. The problems of global environmental pollution, therefore, may get far worse before they get better. The viewpoints in this chapter reflect the varying concerns and opinions about the critical issues of air and water pollution.

Factory Farms Pollute U.S Air and Water Supplies

Natural Resources Defense Council

The Natural Resources Defense Council (NRDC) is an environmental action organization that seeks to protect Earth's wildlife and wild places and ensure a healthy environment.

Factory farms—giant livestock farms also known as feedlots that house thousands of cows, chickens or pigs—produce staggering amounts of animal wastes. The way these wastes are stored and used has profound effects on human health and the environment.

On most factory farms, animals are crowded into relatively small areas; their manure and urine are funneled into massive waste lagoons. These cesspools often break, leak or overflow, sending dangerous microbes, nitrate pollution and drug-resistant bacteria into water supplies. Factory-farm lagoons also emit toxic gases such as ammonia, hydrogen sulfide and methane. What's more, the farms often spray the manure onto land, ostensibly as fertilizer—these "sprayfields" bring still more of these harmful substances into our air and water.

Yet in spite of the huge amounts of animal wastes that factory farms produce, they have largely escaped pollution regulations; loopholes in the law and weak enforcement share the blame. NRDC has fought, and won, a number of courtroom battles over the years to force the federal government to deal with the problem of factory farms, and the U.S. EPA [Environmental Protection Agency] is now under court order to set tighter controls on the release of pathogens into the environment by factory farms, exercise greater oversight on factory

Natural Resources Defense Council, "Pollution from Giant Livestock Farms Threatens Public Health," 2005. www.nrdc.org/water/pollution/nspills.asp. © Natural Resources Defense Council. Reproduced with permission from the Natural Resources Defense Council. This material has been edited for this publication.

farms' pollution-reduction plans, and ensure that these plans are made available to the public.

Threats to Human Health

People who live near or work at factory farms breathe in hundreds of gases, which are formed as manure decomposes. The stench can be unbearable, but worse still, the gases contain many harmful chemicals. For instance, one gas released by the lagoons, hydrogen sulfide, is dangerous even at low levels. Its effects—which are irreversible—range from sore throat to seizures, comas and even death. Other health effects associated with the gases from factory farms include headaches, shortness of breath, wheezing, excessive coughing and diarrhea.

Animal waste also contaminates drinking water supplies. For example, nitrates often seep from lagoons and sprayfields into groundwater. Drinking water contaminated with nitrates can increase the risk of blue baby syndrome, which can cause deaths in infants. High levels of nitrates in drinking water near hog factories have also been linked to spontaneous abortions. Several disease outbreaks related to drinking water have been traced to bacteria and viruses from waste.

On top of this, the widespread use of antibiotics also poses dangers. Large-scale animal factories often give animals antibiotics to promote growth, or to compensate for illness resulting from crowded conditions. These antibiotics are entering the environment and the food chain, contributing to the rise of antibiotic-resistant bacteria and making it harder to treat human diseases.

Threats to the Natural Environment

The natural environment also suffers in many ways from factory-farming practices. Sometimes the damage is sudden and catastrophic, as when a ruptured lagoon causes a massive fish kill. At other times, it is cumulative—for example, when manure is repeatedly overapplied, it runs off the land and accumulates as nutrient pollution in waterways.

Either way, the effects are severe. For instance, water quality across the country is threatened by phosphorus and nitrogen, two nutrients present in animal wastes. In excessive amounts, nutrients often cause an explosion of algae that robs water of oxygen, killing aquatic life. One toxic microorganism, *Pfiesteria piscicida*, has been implicated in the death of more than one billion fish in coastal waters in North Carolina.

Manure can also contain traces of salt and heavy metals, which can end up in bodies of water and accumulate in the sediment, concentrating as they move up the food chain. And lagoons not only pollute groundwater; they also deplete it. Many factory farms use groundwater for cleaning, cooling and providing drinking water.

Better Alternatives Exist

Practical remedies to these problems do exist. But implementing them will require some important changes in factory farm practices and government oversight:

- *Regulation and accountability.* Factory farms are industrial facilities and should be regulated accordingly. They must obtain permits, monitor water quality and pay for cleaning up and disposing of their wastes.

- *Public awareness and participation.* Local governments and residents must have a say in whether to allow factory farms in their communities. The public is also entitled to review and comment on the contents of pollution reduction plans and to enforce the terms, where a factory farm is in violation.

- *New technology.* Factory-farm technology standards must be strengthened. The EPA must consider recent technology advances that significantly reduce pathogens.

- *Alternative farming practices.* States and the federal government should promote methods of raising livestock that reduce the concentration of animals and use manure safely. Many alternative methods exist; they rely on keeping animal waste drier, which limits problems with spills, runoff and air pollution.

- *Pollution-reduction programs for small feedlots.* Voluntary programs must be expanded to encourage smaller factory farms, which fall outside of the regulations for industrial facilities, to improve their management practices and take advantage of available technical assistance and other resources.

- *Consumer pressure.* Individuals can help stop factory farm pollution by supporting livestock farms that use sustainable practices. In the grocery store, this means checking meat labels for "organic," "free range," "antibiotic-free," or similar wording, which indicates meat raised in a more sustainable manner. Many sustainable livestock farms also sell directly to consumers or through local farmers' markets.

Contaminated Water Is Causing Deaths in the Developing World

Nicholas L. Cain and Peter H. Gleick

Nicholas L. Cain is director of communications and Peter H. Gleick is president of the Pacific Institute, an organization dedicated to protecting the natural world, encouraging sustainable development, and improving global security.

People living in the United States or any industrialized nation take safe drinking water for granted. But in much of the developing world, access to clean water is not guaranteed. According to the World Health Organization, more than 1.2 billion people lack access to clean water, and more than 5 million people die every year from contaminated water or water-related diseases.

The Global Water Crisis

The world's nations, through the United Nations (UN), have recognized the critical importance of improving access to clean water and ensuring adequate sanitation and have pledged to cut the proportion of people without such access by half by 2015 as part of the UN Millennium Development Goals. However, even if these goals are reached, tens of millions of people will probably perish from tainted water and water-borne diseases by 2020.

Although ensuring clean water for all is a daunting task, the good news is that the technological know-how exists to treat and clean water and convey it safely. The international

Nicholas L. Cain and Peter H. Gleick, "The Global Water Crisis," *Issues in Science and Technology*, vol. 21, no. 4, summer 2005, pp. 79–81. Copyright 2005 National Academy of Sciences. Reproduced by permission of the Pacific Institute for Studies in Development, Environment, and Security.

aid community and many at-risk nations are already working on a range of efforts to improve access to water and sanitation.

It is clear, however, that more aid will be needed, although the estimates of how much vary widely. There is also considerable debate about the proper mix of larger, more costly projects and smaller, more community-scale projects. Still, it seems that bringing basic water services to the world's poorest people could be done at a reasonable price—probably far less than consumers in developed countries now spend on bottled water.

Despite the toll of the global water crisis, industrial nations spend little on overseas development efforts such as water and sanitation projects.

The global water crisis is a serious threat, and not only to those who suffer, get sick, and die from tainted water or waterborne disease. There is also a growing realization that the water crisis undercuts economic growth in developing nations, can worsen conflicts over resources, and can even affect global security by worsening conditions in states that are close to failure.

Mounting Deaths and Insufficient Aid

According to a Pacific Institute analysis, between 34 million and 76 million people could perish because of contaminated water or water-related diseases by 2020, even if the UN Millennium Development Goals are met.

Despite the toll of the global water crisis, industrial nations spend little on overseas development efforts such as water and sanitation projects. Only 5 of 22 nations have met the modest UN goal of spending 0.7 percent of a nation's gross national income on overseas development assistance. And only a fraction of all international assistance is spent on water and sanitation projects. From 1999 to 2001, an average of only $3 billion annually was provided for water supply and sanitation projects.

Bottled Water

Although tap water, in most of the developed world, is clean and safe, millions of consumers drink bottled water for taste, convenience, or because of worries about water quality. Comprehensive data on bottled water consumption in the developing world are scarce. However, some water experts are worried that increased sales of bottled water to the developing world will reduce pressure on governments to provide basic access to non-bottled water. Others are concerned that the world's poorest people will have to spend a significant amount of their already low incomes to purchase water.

Consumers spend nearly $100 billion annually on bottled water, according to Pacific Institute estimates. Indeed, consumers often pay several hundred to a thousand times as much for bottled water as they do for reliable, high-quality tap water, which costs $.50 per cubic meter in California. This disparity is often worse in developing nations where clean water is far out of reach for the poorest people.

Ozone Depletion and Pollution Are Damaging Human Health and the Environment

U.S. Nuclear Regulatory Commission

The U.S. Nuclear Regulatory Commission (NRC) is an independent agency established by the Energy Reorganization Act of 1974 to regulate civilian use of nuclear materials.

Ozone is a gas that forms in the atmosphere when 3 atoms of oxygen are combined (O_3). It is not emitted directly into the air, but at ground level is created by a chemical reaction between oxides of nitrogen (NO_x), and volatile organic compounds (VOC) in the presence of sunlight. Ozone has the same chemical structure whether it occurs high above the earth or at ground level and can be "good" or "bad," depending on its location in the atmosphere.

How can ozone be both good and bad? Ozone occurs in two layers of the atmosphere. The layer surrounding the earth's surface is the troposphere. Here, ground level or "bad" ozone is an air pollutant that damages human health, vegetation, and many common materials. It is a key ingredient of urban smog. The troposphere extends to a level about 10 miles up, where it meets the second layer, the stratosphere. The stratospheric or "good" ozone layer extends upward from about 10 to 30 miles and protects life on earth from the sun's harmful ultraviolet rays (UV-b).

U.S. Nuclear Regulatory Commission, "Ozone: Good Up High, Bad Nearby," January 2003. www.policyalmanac.org/environment/archive/ozone.shtml. Reproduced by permission.

What Is Happening to the "Good" Ozone Layer?

Ozone occurs naturally in the stratosphere and is produced and destroyed at a constant rate. But this "good" ozone is gradually being destroyed by man-made chemicals called chlorofluorocarbons (CFCs), halons, and other ozone-depleting substances (used in coolants, foaming agents, fire extinguishers, and solvents). These ozone-depleting substances degrade slowly and can remain intact for many years as they move through the troposphere until they reach the stratosphere. There they are broken down by the intensity of the sun's ultraviolet rays and release chlorine and bromine molecules, which destroy "good" ozone. One chlorine or bromine molecule can destroy 100,000 ozone molecules, causing ozone to disappear much faster than nature can replace it.

It can take years for ozone-depleting chemicals to reach the stratosphere, and even though we have reduced or eliminated the use of many CFCs, their impact from years past is just starting to affect the ozone layer. Substances released into the air today will contribute to ozone destruction well into the future.

Increased UV-b can lead to more cases of skin cancer, cataracts, and impaired immune system.

Satellite observations indicate a world-wide thinning of the protective ozone layer. The most noticeable losses occur over the North and South Poles because ozone depletion accelerates in extremely cold weather conditions.

How Does the Depletion of "Good" Ozone Affect Human Health and the Environment?

As the stratospheric ozone layer is depleted, higher UV-b levels reach the earth's surface. Increased UV-b can lead to more cases of skin cancer, cataracts, and impaired immune system.

Damage to UV-b sensitive crops, such as soybeans, reduces yield. High altitude ozone depletion is suspected to cause decreases in phytoplankton, a plant that grows in the ocean. Phytoplankton is an important link in the marine food chain and, therefore, food populations could decline. Because plants "breathe in" carbon dioxide and "breathe out" oxygen, carbon dioxide levels in the air could also increase. Increased UV-b radiation can be instrumental in forming more ground-level or "bad" ozone.

What Is Being Done about the Depletion of Good Ozone?

The Montreal Protocol, a series of international agreements on the reduction and eventual elimination of production and use of ozone-depleting substances, became effective in 1989. Currently, 160 countries participate in the Protocol. Efforts will result in recovery of the ozone layer in about 50 years.

In the United States, the U.S. Environmental Protection Agency (EPA) continues to establish regulations to phase out these chemicals. The Clean Air Act requires warning labels on all products containing CFCs or similar substances, prohibits nonessential ozone-depleting products, and prohibits the release of refrigerants used in car and home air conditioning units and appliances into the air.

What Causes "Bad" Ozone?

Motor vehicle exhaust and industrial emissions, gasoline vapors, and chemical solvents are some of the major sources of NO_x and VOC, also known as ozone precursors. Strong sunlight and hot weather cause ground-level ozone to form in harmful concentrations in the air. Many urban areas tend to have high levels of "bad" ozone, but other areas are also subject to high ozone levels as winds carry NO_x emissions hundreds of miles away from their original sources.

Ozone concentrations can vary from year to year. Changing weather patterns (especially the number of hot, sunny days), periods of air stagnation, and other factors that contribute to ozone formation make long-term predictions difficult.

How Does "Bad" Ozone Affect Human Health and the Environment?

Repeated exposure to ozone pollution may cause permanent damage to the lungs. Even when ozone is present in low levels, inhaling it triggers a variety of health problems including chest pains, coughing, nausea, throat irritation, and congestion. It also can worsen bronchitis, heart disease, emphysema, and asthma, and reduce lung capacity. Healthy people also experience difficulty in breathing when exposed to ozone pollution. Because ozone pollution usually forms in hot weather, anyone who spends time outdoors in the summer may be affected, particularly children, the elderly, outdoor workers and people exercising. Millions of Americans live in areas where the national ozone health standards are exceeded.

Ground-level ozone damages plant life and is responsible for 500 million dollars in reduced crop production in the United States each year. It interferes with the ability of plants to produce and store food, making them more susceptible to disease, insects, other pollutants, and harsh weather. "Bad" ozone damages the foliage of trees and other plants, ruining the landscape of cities, national parks and forests, and recreation areas.

What Is Being Done about Bad Ozone?

The Clean Air Act Amendments of 1990 require EPA, states, and cities to implement programs to further reduce emissions of ozone precursors from sources such as cars, fuels, industrial facilities, power plants, and consumer/commercial products. Power plants will be reducing emissions, cleaner cars and fuels are being developed, many gas stations are using special nozzles at the pumps to recapture gasoline vapors, and vehicle inspection programs are being improved to reduce emissions.

The ultimate responsibility for our environment is our own. Minor lifestyle changes can result in major air quality improvements.

What Can You Do?

High-Altitude "Good" Ozone

- Make sure that technicians working on your car air conditioner, home air conditioner, or refrigerator are certified by an EPA-approved program to recover the refrigerant (this is required by law).

- Have your car and home air conditioner units and refrigerator checked for leaks. When possible, repair leaky air conditioning units before refilling them.

- Contact local authorities to properly dispose of refrigeration or air conditioning equipment.

- Protect yourself against sunburn. Minimize sun exposure during midday hours (10 AM to 4 PM). Wear sunglasses, a hat with a wide brim, and protective clothing with a tight weave. Use a broad spectrum sunscreen with a sun protection factor (SPF) of at least 15, and 30 is better.

Ground-Level "Bad" Ozone

- Keep your automobile well tuned and maintained.

- Carpool, use mass transit, walk, bicycle, and/or reduce driving, especially on hot summer days.

- Be careful not to spill gasoline when filling up your car or gasoline-powered lawn and garden equipment. During the summer, fill your gas tank during the cooler evening hours.

- Make sure your car's tires are properly inflated and your wheels are aligned.

- Participate in your local utility's energy conservation programs.

- Seal containers of household cleaners, workshop chemicals and solvents, and garden chemicals to prevent VOC from evaporating into the air. Dispose of them properly.

We live with ozone every day. It can protect life on earth or harm it, but we have the power to influence ozone's impact by the way we live.

The World's Most Serious Environmental Problem Is Global Warming

Jim Hansen

Jim Hansen is director of the NASA Goddard Institute for Space Studies and an adjunct professor of earth and environmental sciences at Columbia University's Earth Institute.

In Sweden and Norway, the treeline is marching northward and uphill as the snowline recedes. In the Arctic, the polar bear finds its habitat shrinking. Elsewhere in the northern hemisphere, animals are slowly moving north to escape rising temperatures. Behind the silent movement hides a disturbing story that we had better take note of before it is too late. If the present warming trend continues, rising seawater will claim coastal cities all over the world.

The Effect on Animals

Animals have no choice but to move, since their survival is at stake. Recently after appearing on television to discuss climate change, I received an e-mail from a man in northeast Arkansas about his observations of the armadillo: "I had not seen one of these animals my entire life, until the last ten years. I drive the same 40-mile trip on the same road every day and have slowly watched these critters advance further north every year and they are not stopping. Every year they move several miles." The mobility of armadillos suggests that they have a good chance to keep up with the movement of their climate zone, to be one of the surviving species.

Other species have greater problems. Of course, climate [has] fluctuated in the past, yet species adapted and flourished. But now the rate of climate change driven by human activity is reaching a level that dwarfs natural rates of change. If climate change is too great, natural barriers, such as coastlines, spell doom for some species.

Studies of more than 1,000 species of plants, animals, and insects, found an average migration rate toward the North and South Poles of about four miles per decade in the second half of the 20th century. That is not fast enough. During the past 30 years the lines marking the regions in which a given average temperature prevails, or isotherms, have moved poleward at a rate of about 35 miles per decade.

If we continue on this path, a large fraction of the species on Earth, as many as 50 percent or more, may become extinct.

As long as the total movement of isotherms toward the poles is much smaller than the size of the habitat, or the ranges in which the animals live, the effect on species is limited. But now the movement is inexorably toward the poles, totaling more than 100 miles in recent decades. If emissions of greenhouse gases continue to increase at the current rate— "business as usual"—then the rate of isotherm movement will double during [the twenty-first] century to at least 70 miles per decade. If we continue on this path, a large fraction of the species on Earth, as many as 50 percent or more, may become extinct.

The species most at risk are those in polar climates and the biologically diverse slopes of alpine regions, [which will be] literally pushed off the planet. A few species, such as polar bears, no doubt will be "rescued" by human beings, but survival in zoos or reserves will be small consolation to bears or nature lovers.

In the Earth's history, during periods when average global temperatures increased by as much as 10 degrees Fahrenheit, there have been several "mass extinctions," when between 50 and 90 percent of the species on Earth disappeared forever. In each case, life survived and new species developed over hundreds of thousands of years—but the life that survived was dramatically different from that which dominated before. The most recent of these mass extinctions defines the boundary, 55 million years ago, between the Paleocene and Eocene epochs. The evolutionary turmoil associated with that climate change gave rise to a host of modern mammals, from rodents to primates, which appear in fossil records for the first time in the early Eocene.

The greatest threat of climate change for human beings lies in the potential destabilization of the massive ice sheets in Greenland and Antarctica.

If human beings follow a business-as-usual course, continuing to exploit fossil fuel resources without reducing carbon emissions or capturing and sequestering them before they warm the atmosphere, the eventual effects on climate and life may be comparable to those at the time of mass extinctions. Life will survive, but on a transformed planet. For foreseeable human generations, the world will be far more desolate than the one in which civilization flourished during the past several thousand years.

The Threat to Humans

The greatest threat of climate for human beings lies in the potential destabilization of the massive ice sheets in Greenland and Antarctica, a catastrophe that would be as irreversible as the extinction of species. Future rise in the sea level depends, dramatically, on the increase in greenhouse gases, which will largely determine the amount of global warming.

To arrive at an effective policy we can project two scenarios concerning climate change. In the business-as-usual scenario, annual emissions of CO_2 continue to increase at the current rate for at least 50 years. In the alternative scenario, CO_2 emissions level off this decade [2001–2010], slowly decline for a few decades, and by mid-century decrease rapidly, aided by new technologies. The business-as-usual scenario yields an increase of about 5 degrees Fahrenheit of global warming during this century, while the alternative scenario yields an increase of less than 2 degrees Fahrenheit during the same period.

The last time that the Earth was five degrees warmer was 3 million years ago, when the sea level was about 80 feet higher. In that case, the world would lose Shanghai, Tokyo, Amsterdam, Venice and New York. In the US, 50 million people live below that sea level. China would have 250 million displaced persons. Bangladesh would produce 120 million refugees, practically the entire nation. India would lose the land of 150 million people.

A rise in sea level, necessarily, begins slowly. Massive ice sheets soften before rapid disintegration and melting occurs and sea level rises. The Earth's history reveals cases in which sea level, once ice sheets began to collapse, rose 1 meter every 20 years for centuries, [a] calamity for hundreds of cities throughout the world. Satellite images and other data have revealed the initial response of ice sheets to global warming. The area on Greenland in which summer melting of ice took place increased more than 50 percent during the last 25 years. The volume of icebergs from Greenland has doubled in the last 10 years.

The effect of this loss of ice on the global sea level is small so far, but accelerating. The likelihood of the sudden collapse of ice sheets increases as global warming continues. For example, wet ice is darker; thus, as ice sheets continue to melt they absorb more sunlight and melt even faster.

The business-as-usual scenario, with 5 degrees Fahrenheit global warming and 10 degrees Fahrenheit at the ice sheets, would certainly lead to their disintegration. The only question is when the collapse will begin. The business-as-usual scenario, which could lead to an eventual sea level rise of 80 feet, with 20 feet or more per century, could produce global chaos, leaving fewer resources with which to mitigate the change in climate. The alternative scenario, with global warming under 2 degrees Fahrenheit, still produces a rise in the sea level, but the slower rate allows time to develop strategies for adapting to the changes.

The Earth's creatures, save for one species, do not have thermostats in their living rooms that they can adjust for an optimum environment. But people—those with thermostats— must take notice, and turn down the world's thermostat before it is too late.

Carbon Dioxide Emissions That Cause Global Warming Are Increasing

Space Daily

Space Daily *is a daily online news service for the space industry.*

According to the co-Chair of the Global Carbon Project, CSIRO [Australia's Commonwealth Scientific and Industrial Research Organisation] Marine and Atmospheric Research scientist Dr. Mike Raupach, 7.9 billion tonnes [8.7 U.S. tons] of carbon were emitted into the atmosphere as carbon dioxide in 2005 and the rate of increase is accelerating. "From 2000 to 2005, the growth rate of carbon dioxide emissions was more than 2.5 percent per year, whereas in the 1990s it was less than one percent per year," Dr. Raupach says. He says this indicates that recent efforts globally to reduce emissions have had little impact on emissions growth. "Recent emissions seem to be near the high end of the fossil fuel use scenarios used by the Intergovernmental Panel on Climate Change (IPCC). On our current path, it will be difficult to rein-in carbon emissions enough to stabilise the atmospheric carbon dioxide concentration at 450 ppm [parts per million]."

Sources of Emissions

Dr. Raupach's figures show that while China demonstrates the highest current growth rate in emissions, its emissions per person are still below the global average and its accumulated contribution since the start of the industrial revolution around 1800 is only five percent of the global total. This compares to the US and Europe, which have each contributed more than 25 percent of accumulated global emissions.

Space Daily, "Increase in Carbon Dioxide Emissions Accelerating," November 30, 2006. Copyright 2006 *Space Daily*. Distributed by United Press International. Reproduced by permission.

Dr. Raupach says that the amount of emitted carbon dioxide remaining in the atmosphere fluctuates from year to year due to natural factors such as El Niño. However, he says that on average, nearly half of all emissions from fossil fuel use and land-use changes remain in the atmosphere, with the rest being absorbed by the land and oceans. "When natural variability is smoothed out, 45 percent of emissions have remained in the atmosphere each year over the past 50 years," he say. "A danger is that the land and oceans might take up less carbon dioxide in the future than they have in the past, which would increase the rate of climate change caused by emissions."

Unprecedented Growth

The latest findings on greenhouse gas emissions are supported by measurements of the subsequent concentrations of carbon dioxide in the atmosphere. Dr. Paul Fraser, also from CSIRO Marine and Atmospheric Research, says that atmospheric concentrations of carbon dioxide grew by two parts per million in 2005, the fourth year in a row of above-average growth. "To have four years in a row of above-average carbon dioxide growth is unprecedented," Dr. Fraser says.

Dr. Fraser says the 30-year record of air collected, at the Australian Bureau of Meteorology's observation station in Cape Grim, showed growth rates of just over one part per million in the early 1980s, but in recent years carbon dioxide has increased at almost twice this rate. "The trend over recent years suggests the growth rate is accelerating, signifying that fossil fuels are having an impact on greenhouse gas concentrations in a way we haven't seen in the past."

U.S. Air Quality Has Improved Since the 1970s

Ronald Bailey

Ronald Bailey is an award-winning science correspondent for Reason, *a monthly libertarian magazine.*

When I talk about environmental trends at colleges, I often start with a question: "Has air pollution in the United States gotten worse or better over the past three decades?" The majority—often a vast majority—of my audience will raise their hands in favor of the proposition that air quality has gotten worse. Polls consistently show that most Americans would join them in agreeing with that—completely false—notion.

The Good News

A . . . study from air quality analyst Joel Schwartz does a great job spelling out the good news about air pollution, and explaining why the good news will get better. *No Way Back: Why Air Pollution Will Continue to Decline* [was] released by the American Enterprise Institute (AEI) [in 2003]. Schwartz debuted his analysis in a timely presentation at AEI the day before Earth Day. Such good news about environmental trends is, alas, strangely rare during the annual celebration of environmental awareness—and environmental fearmongering.

Using uncontroversial data from agencies like the U.S. Environmental Protection Agency (EPA) and the California Air Resources Board, Schwartz shows that air pollution news has been good across the board for decades now. Since the mid-1960s the best available measurements show that sulfur dioxide levels have fallen by more than 80 percent, carbon monox-

Ronald Bailey, "Clearing the Air: An Earth Day Celebration," *ReasonOnline*, April 22, 2003. www.reason.com/news/show/34800.html. Reproduced by permission.

ide levels are down more than 75 percent, nitrogen dioxide levels dropped over 40 percent, ozone levels decreased nearly 50 percent, and the level of total particulates (smoke, soot, dust) is down by more than 60 percent.

In the 1980s, the EPA also started measuring smaller particles in the air, which are believed to have graver health consequences than some of those older pollution markers. Levels of those tiny terrors have declined nearly 30 percent. By almost any standard, air quality greatly improved between 1970 and 2000, even as [the] U.S. population grew by 39 percent, energy use increased by 42 percent, total vehicle miles driven jumped by 143 percent, and gross domestic product soared by 149 percent.

There is no connection any longer between increased population, industrial production, energy consumption, or car use and increased air pollution.

More Improvement Likely in the Future

There is no connection any longer between increased population, industrial production, energy consumption, or car use and increased air pollution. The already low air pollution levels in the United States will inevitably drop much further over the next two decades. As Schwartz explains, "most future pollution reductions will come from things we have already done." New technologies and regulations already put in place will continue to clear our air.

New cars already pollute far less than older cars, so as older cars are replaced by cleaner new cars, the air will continue to clear. "Almost all pollution from gasoline-powered vehicles will disappear over the next 20 years," Schwartz declares. Simply by implementing the standards now on the books and through the normal process of automobile fleet turnover, total average emissions from all autos will decline by at least another 85 percent over the next two decades. While most of the improvements in air quality are the result of regulations, Schwartz notes that even when enforced air quality standards did not change between 1982 and 1992, the amount of pollutants emitted by automobiles continued to decline each year, probably as a result of improved air and fuel mixing technologies in newer cars.

Some environmentalists fear that the effects of "suburban sprawl" and increasing numbers of gas-guzzling SUVs will halt the progress in reducing air pollution. But Schwartz notes that as the percentage of SUVs grew from 31 percent to 38 percent and gasoline use increased by 12 percent in California between 1994 and 2001, total emissions still continued their steep drops. Hydrocarbons were down by more than 60 percent, nitrogen oxides by over 40 percent, and carbon monoxide by 55 percent.

Of course past performance is no guarantee of future results, as we've all learned from the stock market. So to account for the increasing popularity of SUVs and more miles traveled, Schwartz's analysis assumed that gasoline consumption would rise over the next 20 years at 2 percent per year. In recent years gas consumption has only increased by around 1.7 percent annually. Based on that assumption, what would have been a 90 percent decline in the emissions rate becomes an 85 percent reduction—not a new air pollution crisis by any means.

Cheap Solution for Even Cleaner Air

"The vast majority of health benefits from reduced air pollution have already been achieved in most of the U.S.," Schwartz says. But if we want even cleaner air faster, there are a couple of relatively cheap things we can do now. First, get the most polluting cars off the road. Between 45 and 60 percent of smog precursors are emitted by just 5 percent of the cars on the road. These hyperpolluters could be detected using remote sensing technologies and their owners offered money to scrap them. Second, policy makers should eschew any policy that makes new cars more expensive.

For example, a proposal to raise the prices of conventional cars and use the extra money to lower the prices of electric cars—which are estimated to cost $17,000 more than conventional cars—would be counterproductive. Since new conventional cars will be virtually pollution-free soon, raising their prices will have the perverse effect of encouraging drivers to hold on to their older, more polluting jalopies longer, thus increasing overall emissions.

In the face of the overwhelming evidence to the contrary, why do the majority of Americans still believe that air pollution is getting worse? When crime rates fall, mayors, police chiefs, and district attorneys are eager to spread the news and take the credit. But when pollution levels fall, environmentalists and environmental bureaucrats show a peculiar reluctance to cheer. Schwartz suggests that the difference is that the environmental movement uses scare stories to raise money for their campaigns: no crisis, no money, no movement. In other words, Americans believe that air pollution is getting worse because some people make a living peddling that misinformation.

The bottom line, says Schwartz: "Not only will air pollution not increase, there's virtually no way to stop large decreases in air pollution in the future." That's Earth Day news worth celebrating.

U.S. Rivers, Streams, and Groundwater Are Generally Healthy

U.S. Geological Survey

The U.S. Geological Survey (USGS) is a federal agency that provides scientific information about the natural sciences to help manage the nation's water, biological, energy, and mineral resources.

The U.S. Geological Survey National Water-Quality Assessment (NAWQA) Program released the last 15 of 51 reports on water quality in major river basins and aquifers across the Nation [in 2004]. NAWQA began assessing the quality of our streams, ground water, and aquatic ecosystems in 1991. Collectively, the new reports characterize the general health of our ground- and surface-water resources, address current and emerging water issues and priorities, and describe trends in water quality—a wealth of information that contributes to practical and effective water-resource management. Selected findings of regional and national interest are highlighted in a separate report, "Water Quality in the Nation's Streams and Aquifers—Overview of Selected Findings, 1991–2001."

U.S. Waters Are Safe

NAWQA assessments indicate that the Nation's waters generally are suitable for irrigation, drinking-water supply, and other home and recreational uses. Major challenges that continue to affect streams and ground water in parts of every study unit include point and nonpoint sources of pesticides, nutrients, metals, gasoline-related compounds, and other contaminants.

U.S. Geological Survey, "New Reports on Our Nation's Water Quality" (Fact Sheet 2004–3045), U.S. Geological Survey, Department of the Interior/USGS U.S. Geological Survey, May 2004. http://pubs.usgs.gov/fs/2004/3045/. Reproduced by permission.

These assessments use a nationally consistent design and methodology so that water-resource managers can compare water quality in their basins to other areas in the Nation. The assessments also delineate the effects of natural factors and human activities on water resources, such as effects associated with agriculture and urban development. Contaminant levels vary from season to season and among watersheds because of differences in land and chemical use, land-management practices, degree of watershed development, and natural features, such as soils, geology, hydrology, and climate. Using this information, decision makers can implement cost-effective water-management strategies in specific geographic areas.

Selected Highlights from NAWQA Reports

Changes in land management can improve stream-water quality. For example, best management practices that began in the 1990s in much of the Yakima River Basin, Washington (such as converting from rill, or "furrow," irrigation to sprinkler and drip irrigation), have reduced runoff from farm fields, thus reducing suspended sediment, total phosphorus, dissolved nitrate, and organochlorine compounds (such as DDT) in streams. Concentrations of total DDT (DDT and its stable breakdown products) in largescale suckers, smallmouth bass, and carp from the lower Yakima River decreased by about half from the late 1980s to 1998.

Ground-water quality also responds to changes in land management, but usually more slowly than surface water. USGS ground-water age-dating techniques used on the Delmarva Peninsula (Delaware, Maryland, and Virginia) indicate that improvements in ground-water quality, including reduced concentrations of nitrate from agricultural fertilizers, can lag behind land-management changes by decades because of the slow rate of ground-water flow.

Urbanizing watersheds show positive and negative changes in water quality. NAWQA sampled sediment cores from 42 reservoirs and lakes in 20 metropolitan areas across the Nation from 1996 to 2001, including near Chicago, Los Angeles, Salt Lake City, and Newark. Data show decreasing concentrations of lead, PCBs, and DDT since their use was restricted in the 1970s, whereas polycyclic aromatic hydrocarbons (PAHs) generally are increasing in urbanizing watersheds with increased motor vehicle traffic.

Some contaminants occur naturally, even in relatively pristine areas like the Yellowstone River Basin in Wyoming and Montana.

Even low levels of urbanization can affect aquatic ecosystems, as shown by stream-ecology studies in the Anchorage, Birmingham, Boston, Chicago, Dayton-Cincinnati, Los Angeles, Philadelphia-Trenton, and Salt Lake City metropolitan areas. . . .

The influence of natural features can be substantial. For example, mercury concentrations are affected by the amount of wetlands and the presence of sulfur, carbon, organic matter, and dissolved oxygen in the soils and water. Concentrations of total mercury were higher in sediment in urban watersheds in the Boston metropolitan area than in adjacent, more forested watersheds in Maine and New Hampshire; however, concentrations of total mercury in fish (most of which was the most toxic form, methylmercury) were higher in fish in the forested watersheds, in large part because of the larger amount of wetlands.

NAWQA analyses detect very low levels of pesticides and volatile organic compounds (VOCs). There was widespread detection of these compounds, albeit often at low concentrations, in river basins and aquifer systems across a wide range of landscapes and land uses. In the mostly agricultural Lower Tennessee River Basin, for example, 52 different pesticides were detected in streams and rivers, and VOCs were detected in about 67 percent of sampled springs and wells that tap underlying carbonate aquifers.

Streams and ground water in watersheds with significant agriculture or urban development usually contain mixtures of VOCs, nutrients, pesticides, and their chemical breakdown products. In Oahu, for example, VOCs and pesticides were detected together in more than half of sampled public-supply wells, with one exception. Few contaminants were detected in Honolulu due to a century of urban planning and watershed protection that directs intensive chemical use and storage away from upland recharge areas of the city.

Some contaminants occur naturally, even in relatively pristine areas like the Yellowstone River Basin in Wyoming and Montana. Elevated concentrations of phosphorus in streams are derived from igneous and marine sedimentary rocks; elevated concentrations of arsenic most likely result from sedimentary rocks in contact with geothermal waters.

Earth's Stratospheric Ozone Layer Is Recovering

Jane Sanders

Jane Sanders is the editor of Research Horizons, *a magazine published by the Georgia Institute of Technology.*

Concentrations of atmospheric ozone—which protects Earth from the sun's ultraviolet radiation—are showing signs of recovery in the most important regions of the stratosphere above the mid-latitudes in both the Northern and Southern hemispheres, a new study shows. Researchers attribute the improvement to both a reduction in ozone-depleting chemicals phased out by the global Montreal Protocol treaty and its amendments and to changes in atmospheric transport dynamics. The study, funded by NASA [the National Aeronautics and Space Administration], is the first to document a difference among stratospheric regions in ozone-level improvement and to establish a cause-and-effect relationship based on direct measurements by multiple satellite and ground-based, ozone-monitoring systems.

"We do think we're on the road to recovery of stratospheric ozone, but what we don't know is exactly how that recovery will happen," said Derek Cunnold, a professor of earth and atmospheric sciences at the Georgia Institute of Technology. "Many in the scientific community think it will be at least 50 years before ozone levels return to the pre-1980 levels when ozone began to decline."

The research results [were] published Sept. 9, 2006, in the American Geophysical Union's *Journal of Geophysical Research—Atmospheres.* Georgia Tech research scientist Eun-Su

Yang led the study in close collaboration with Cunnold, Ross Salawitch of NASA's Jet Propulsion Laboratory at the California Institute of Technology, M. Patrick McCormick and James Russell III of Hampton University, Joseph Zawodny of NASA Langley Research Center, Samuel Oltmans of the NOAA [National Oceanic and Atmospheric Administration] Earth System Research Laboratory and Professor Mike Newchurch at the University of Alabama in Huntsville.

Atmospheric ozone has stopped decreasing in one region and is actually increasing in the other of the two most important lower regions of the stratosphere.

The Study's Findings

The study's data indicate that atmospheric ozone has stopped decreasing in one region and is actually increasing in the other of the two most important lower regions of the stratosphere. Scientists attribute the stabilization of ozone levels in the past decade in the 11- to 15-mile (18- to 25-kilometer) altitude region to the Montreal Protocol, enacted in 1987, and its amendments. The treaty phased out the use of ozone-depleting chemicals, including chlorofluorocarbons (CFCs) emitted from such sources as spray-can propellants, refrigerator coolants and foam insulation.

In the 7- to 11-mile (11- to 18-kilometer) region, the researchers link a slight increase in ozone to changes in atmospheric transport—perhaps caused by natural variability or human-induced climate warming—rather than atmospheric chemistry. The changes in this altitude range—below the region where ozone-depleting gases derived from human activity are thought to cause ozone depletion—contribute about half of the overall-measured improvement, researchers said.

"There is now widespread agreement in the scientific community that ozone is leveling off in the 18- to 25-kilometer region of the stratosphere because of the Montreal Protocol," Cunnold said. "And we believe there is some tendency toward an increase in ozone in this region, though further study is needed to be certain.

"In the 11- to 18-kilometer region, ozone is definitely increasing because of changes in atmospheric dynamics and transport not related to the Montreal Protocol," he added. "But we don't know the long-term effect this change will have in this region."

Other Studies

Other recent studies complement these new findings. Among them are a study published in 2003 in the *Journal of Geophysical Research*, which reported a slowdown in the ozone depletion rate in the upper stratosphere at about 22 to 28 miles altitude (35 to 45 kilometers). Newchurch at the University of Alabama in Huntsville led this study in collaboration with: Cunnold, his former Ph.D. advisor, Yang, his former Ph.D. student; and other prominent scientists. Newchurch is also an author on the [September 9, 2006,] paper.

The Montreal Protocol—the first major global agreement related to atmospheric change—is working.

More recently, a study published in the journal *Nature* on May 3, 2006, indicated a stabilization and slight increase in the total-column stratospheric ozone in the past decade. This work, led by Betsy Weatherhead at the University of Colorado at Boulder, relied on satellite and ground-based ozone data used in 14 modeling studies done by researchers around the world. She and her colleagues also attributed the changes to the Montreal Protocol, but could not separate treaty-related changes from transport-related changes because of limited information available on ozone variations by height.

Methodology of the Recent Study

In the current study, Yang, Cunnold and their co-authors reached their conclusions based on satellite and ground-based atmospheric ozone measurements. They analyzed a tremendous amount of data from three extremely accurate NASA satellite instruments (SAGE I and II and HALOE) that began collecting data in 1979 and continued until 2005, with the exception of a three-year period in the early 1980s. Ground-based ozone measurements taken by NASA and NOAA from 1979 to 2005 and balloons provided essential complementary data for the study, Yang said. The satellites and the balloons measured ozone levels by atmospheric region. The ground-based data recorded measurements for the total ozone column. "The ground-based measurements were especially important for the lower atmosphere because satellites can have difficulty in sensing the lowest regions," Yang said.

Salawitch, a senior research scientist at NASA's Jet Propulsion Laboratory, noted: "Our study provides a quantitative measure of a key fingerprint that is lacking in earlier studies—the response of the ozone layer as function of height. We reconcile the height-dependent response with observations from other instruments that record variations in total-column ozone."

To accurately attribute the ozone level changes to the Montreal Protocol, researchers had to account for long- and short-term natural fluctuations in ozone concentration, Cunnold noted. One such fluctuation is an 11-year solar cycle, and another is a two-year oscillation that occurs in the tropics, but affects ozone in other latitudes because of atmospheric transport. Despite the natural fluctuations, Yang, Cunnold and their co-authors are very confident in the conclusions they reached from the data they analyzed. "We know from the study we've just published that the Montreal Protocol—the first major global agreement related to atmospheric change—is working," Cunnold said.

A new NASA satellite called Aura is continuing to measure ozone in various regions of the stratosphere, and these same researchers are involved in the ongoing study of the ozone layer using the satellite's data.

CHAPTER 2

Are Corporations Polluting the Environment?

Chapter Preface

Businesses specializing in products that are environmentally friendly and do not pollute, often called "green" or eco-businesses, have grown tremendously since the mid-1990s. Increasingly, U.S. consumers are buying green products that are manufactured without harming the environment or that seek to reduce pollution levels. Evidence of this trend can be seen in several areas. Sales of hybrid cars, for example, which typically combine a standard internal combustion engine with an electric motor powered by batteries, increased from about 9,000 in 2002 to above 200,000 in 2005, according to Hybridcars.com. More and more people have also sought out green building products and services. The U.S. Green Building Council has reported that sales of these green construction items nearly doubled from $5.8 billion in 2003 to $10 billion in 2005.

By far the largest green industry, however, is organic foods—agricultural and meat products that are produced to minimize pollution to air, water, and soil. Organic crops, for example, are grown without using chemical pesticides, artificial fertilizers, or sewage sludge, and processed without using radiation or food additives. Organic meats are produced without antibiotics or growth hormones, and are not genetically modified. In the United States, to earn an "organic" label, producers must manufacture and handle food items according to regulations developed by the U.S. Department of Agriculture (USDA) under the Organic Food Production Act of 1990. The U.S. standard is that the product must be at least 95 percent organic. Other countries, such as the United Kingdom and Australia, have their own organic standards. Although organic food makes up only about 2.4 percent of the overall food industry, it is rapidly increasing in size. Organic food sales have grown at least 15 percent per year since 1992, compared to a growth rate of only about 2–3 percent for conventionally grown foods.

Organic foods, and many other green businesses in the United States, have their roots in the 1960s and 1970s when some young people in the counterculture and anti–Vietnam War movement rejected conventional lifestyles and started "hippie" farms and communes that sought to produce food and other items naturally and ecologically, without polluting the environment. As years passed, the publicity surrounding various food scares involving conventionally grown foods, such as high pesticide levels, *E. coli* food poisoning, and mad cow disease, helped to expand the demand for organic products by mainstream consumers. In the 1990s and more recently, consumers' interest in healthy lifestyles and gourmet cooking has further popularized organic food.

Once, organic foods could be found only at farmers markets or in small, specialty organic stores. The next phase of the industry's growth came with the establishment of large natural foods supermarket chains, such as Whole Foods and Wild Oats, which carry large amount of organic foods and other green products and sell to a largely upscale clientele. Today, many traditional major supermarkets also carry organic along with nonorganic produce. In fact, in 2006, Wal-Mart, the nation's largest retailer, announced that it would carry a larger volume of organic food in its 2,000 supercenters. Wal-Mart may soon become the nation's largest seller of organic food.

Wal-Mart's decision to go organic caused both praise and concern among organic food supporters. Although organic foods typically cost much more than nonorganic foods, Wal-Mart indicated that it would price organic foods no more than 10 percent higher than its conventional produce. Because of the company's size and clout, and its business tactic of forcing down the prices of goods, some people worried that

Wal-Mart would force suppliers to take shortcuts that could lower the quality of organic products. Other observers, however, applauded the Wal-Mart announcement, predicting that the company would bring organic food to an even broader market, especially smaller communities that do not have access to other good sources of organic produce.

Indeed, if demand for organic foods expands, organic foods could move from a niche product to big business, and food manufacturers will strive to produce for that market. Already, major food suppliers such as Kellogg, Kraft, General Mills, and Pepsico are working to create organic versions of their most popular products for Wal-Mart. If this trend develops, more land will likely be devoted to chemical-free organic agriculture, which will mean a corresponding reduction of agricultural pollution—a result that can only be good for the environment. As Wal-Mart chief executive Lee Scott said in a July 2006 *Fortune* magazine article, "There can't be anything good about putting all these chemicals in the air. There can't be anything good about the smog you see in the cities. Those things are just inherently wrong, whether you are an environmentalist or not."

Businesses that produce green products, however, are still only a tiny part of the U.S. and world economy. The authors in this chapter provide information about how other, more traditional businesses are responding to pollution and environmental regulation.

America's Largest Carbon-Dioxide-Emitting Companies Lag Behind Foreign Companies in Addressing Global Warming

Douglas G. Cogan

Douglas G. Cogan is deputy director of the Social Issues Service, part of the Investor Responsibility Research Center (IRRC), a research and consulting firm on corporate governance and social responsibility. He has written several reports on environmental and energy topics.

This report is the first comprehensive examination of how 100 of the world's largest corporations are positioning themselves to compete in a carbon-constrained world. With the launch of the Kyoto Protocol in 2005, managing greenhouse gas emissions is now a routine part of doing business in key global trading markets. As the United States moves to join the international effort to combat global warming, climate governance practices will assume an increasingly central role in corporate and investment planning. Eventually, nothing short of an energy and technology revolution will be needed to stem rising greenhouse gas emissions across the globe.

Faced with record warmth, unprecedented hurricane activity and rapid shrinking of polar ice caps, industry opposition to confronting climate change is diminishing. Skeptics no longer question whether human activity is warming the globe, but how fast. Companies at the vanguard no longer question how much it will cost to reduce greenhouse gas emissions, but how much money they can make doing it. Financial markets are starting to reward companies that are moving ahead on climate change, while those lagging behind are being assigned more risk.

Ultimately, effective corporate responses to climate change must be built on well-functioning environmental management systems and properly focused governance practices. Shareholders and financial analysts will increasingly assign value to companies that prepare for and capitalize on business opportunities posed by climate change—whether from greenhouse gas (GHG) regulations, direct physical impacts or changes in corporate reputation. . . .

U.S. Companies: Progress Since 2003

The first edition of this report, published in 2003 . . . scored 20 global companies on 14 governance actions that companies should take to proactively address the climate issue. A key finding of that report was that major American companies and industries were largely ignoring or discounting climate change in their governance practices and strategic planning. This is no longer the case. Corporate leaders in many industries have begun to meet the climate challenge. Consider the following:

- In 2003, U.S.-based petroleum companies had virtually a single-minded focus on oil and gas development. *In 2004, Chevron formally integrated renewable technologies into its energy portfolio, and now invest more than $100 million per year in low-carbon and carbon-free energy alternatives.*

- In 2003, U.S. auto companies relied on sales of big sport utility vehicles [SUVs] with low gas mileage as their main source of profits. *In 2004, Ford introduced the first American-built hybrid SUV, and now plans to increase hybrid vehicle production tenfold, to 250,000 annually, by 2010.*

- In 2003, few U.S. electric power companies acknowledged the risks related to climate change. *In 2004, American Electric Power announced plans to build the first commercial-scale power plant using coal gasification technology, calling it the "right investment" given foreseeable GHG regulations. Cinergy and many other companies are indicating that GHG regulations are likely and are now advocating for a national climate policy with mandatory controls.*

- In 2003, American equipment manufacturers were largely silent about their plans to develop GHG-saving technologies. *In 2005, General Electric launched its "eco-magination" campaign, a plan to double investments in climate-friendly technologies and reach $20 billion in annual sales by 2010.*

For all of the positive steps that American companies are taking to address climate change . . . , most are playing catch up with their international competitors.

The U.S. companies profiled in this report, covering 10 different industries, provide many positive examples of actions that companies are taking to integrate climate change in their governance practices and strategic planning. This report examines five such topics in detail.

- *Board oversight:* Companies like Anadarko Petroleum, Cinergy and Dow Chemical have created climate change task forces to integrate board oversight with executive-level actions to manage greenhouse gas emissions.

- *Management execution*: The CEOs of companies like Alcoa, Duke Power and United Technologies have become leaders in their industries by articulating the business case for GHG controls and a supportive government regulatory framework.

- *Public disclosure*: Companies like DuPont, Ford and Entergy have disclosed their climate risks and opportunities in their securities filings and other public documents.

- *Emissions accounting*: Companies like General Motors, Southern and Sunoco have provided detailed public accounts of their GHG emissions that include historical baselines, tracking of emissions savings and projections of future trends.

- *Strategic planning*: Companies like Air Products & Chemicals, Edison International and Weyerhaeuser have created business management and product development plans which are poised to seize new opportunities presented by climate change.

American Companies Lag Behind Foreign Competitors

For all of the positive steps that American companies are taking to address climate change at the governance level, most are playing catch up with their international competitors—companies such as BP [British Petroleum], Toyota, Alcan, Unilever and Rio Tinto. . . .

Such international leadership is partly because these non-U.S. companies are based in countries that have ratified the Kyoto Protocol and have begun to implement greenhouse gas emission controls. However, because many U.S. firms also compete in these markets and are subject to the same regulations, geography alone does not account for all of these differences. Other company-specific factors, such as integration of board and management environmental roles, long-term planning cycles and a commitment to sustainability reporting, typically contribute to the industry-leading positions of many non-U.S. companies.

This report also identifies a handful of industry groups—especially coal, food product and airline companies—where climate change continues to be widely ignored as a governance priority, even though it could have a tremendous impact on their business. For example, many coal companies (especially in the U.S.) have done little to mitigate the financial impacts of carbon regulations, despite managing the world's most carbon intensive fuel source. Similarly, food product companies have agricultural-based raw materials and water resources at risk, but few have developed a strategy to manage this exposure. And while airline companies are among the world's fastest growing sources of CO_2 emissions, they have the lowest average governance scores among all 10 sectors examined, in part because they are looking mainly to other industries to find technological solutions and achieve emissions improvements.

Businesses are at risk from the physical impacts of climate change, including the increased intensity and frequency of weather events.

Characteristics of Leading Companies

While climate change should be a governance focus of all companies and major industry groups, the risks and opportunities presented by this issue are not distributed evenly. Some companies and industries—by virtue of the types and amount of energy they use or produce—will be better positioned to respond than others. Likewise, some companies and industries—by virtue of the types and location of their businesses and physical assets—will be more vulnerable to changing climatic conditions.

Among leadership companies, however, three common governance practices should serve as a model for all firms, regardless of the risk-reward ratio that climate change presents to their particular circumstances. At these leading firms:

- *Boards of directors and senior executives work together to address climate change and other sustainability issues.* A key challenge for all firms is ensuring that boards are adequately prepared and empowered to focus on GHG reduction and climate mitigation strategies.

- *CEOs embrace climate change as a near-term priority.* True leaders are speaking out on climate policy, risks and opportunities, rather than leaving the issue to their successors.

- *Management teams pursue practical solutions to climate change.* Rather than waiting for breakthrough technologies, management teams are working to find cost-effective, near-term ways to reduce GHG emissions, starting with energy conservation and more efficient production processes. At the same time, many of these companies are laying the building blocks toward a carbon-neutral economy, with projects focused on carbon sequestration and infrastructure for hydrogen fuels. . . .

Why Companies Must Act Now

Given the sweeping global nature of climate change, climate risk has become embedded, to a greater or lesser extent, in every business and investment portfolio. Companies with significant GHG emissions or energy-intensive operations face risks from new regulations. Climate change also poses direct physical risks to a wide array of firms and industries. Climate change deserves discussion in securities filings in the many instances in which direct financial risks or opportunities can be identified.

Physical Risks: Businesses are at risk from the physical impacts of climate change, including the increased intensity and frequency of weather events, droughts, floods, storms and sea level rise. Changes in consumer habits that accompany changing weather patterns will also affect profitability in a number of sectors. . . . After Hurricane Katrina [for example], one of the strongest hurricanes on record, New Orleans remains a city in disrepair. Businesses along the Gulf Coast suffered billions of dollars of infrastructure damage, with particularly costly effects to oil and gas rigs and refineries. Forecasters are predicting another very active hurricane season in the months ahead. . . .

State, national, and international regulations are putting increasing pressure on companies with emissions.

All told, trillions of dollars of property on or near coastlines now stands in harm's way. Away from the coasts, drought and more frequent heat waves could lead to the collapse of local food systems. According to the World Meteorological Organization, the percentage of the Earth's land area stricken by severe drought has already more than doubled over the last quarter century.

Regulatory Risk: State, national, and international regulations are putting increasing pressure on companies with emissions from operations or products to invest in emissions controls, purchase carbon credits, or face clean-up costs. In the United Kingdom and throughout Europe, as well as in Canada and Japan, the Kyoto Protocol has come into effect. Developing countries like China also have emission reduction laws in place. Compliance with global emission reduction requirements is likely to be significantly more costly for companies with the poorest climate governance.

Nationally, it is only a matter of time before Congress enacts federal carbon constraints. . . . In the face of federal inaction, regulatory activity is picking up at the state and regional level. California and ten other states are moving to limit CO_2 emissions from automobiles. This would impact at least 33 percent of all new cars and light trucks sold in the U.S. Likewise, four states are already regulating CO_2 from electric utilities, and others are considering it. Seven northeastern states have agreed to a cap-and-trade emissions reduction program for the electric power sector, and California, Oregon, and Washington are working on a similar region-wide approach to limit greenhouse gases.

Competitive Risk: Tightly linked to regulatory risk in the global and domestic marketplaces, climate risk preparedness will be a key driver in a company's ability to compete. At present, Ford and General Motors are engaged in a high-stakes struggle to remain competitive as customers turn away from gas-guzzling SUVs in favor of hybrids and other vehicles from Japanese competitors. In China, auto sales are surging well beyond growth rates that the U.S. market has seen in recent decades. However, only 19 percent of current U.S. passenger cars and 14 percent of light-duty trucks can meet China's 2008 emission standards. Both Toyota and Honda have decided to introduce their highly fuel-efficient hybrid models in the burgeoning Chinese market....

Technological and Competitive Risks and Opportunities: Companies in many sectors can increase profitability by implementing energy efficiency strategies and developing emission-reducing technologies or new products that meet changing corporate and consumer demands. Fossil fuels have been the driver of economic growth for more than two centuries, but change is clearly afoot. Global investments in renewable energy hit a record $30 billion in 2004, providing 1.7 million jobs worldwide. Far larger investments are expected in the years ahead, as Europe, the U.S., China and Japan aggressively embrace solar, wind and other climate-friendly options over increasingly costly fuels like oil and natural gas....

In short, the stakes could not be higher for U.S. companies and investors. The greatest investment opportunities as this new era takes hold will lie with companies that capitalize on this emerging shift in global energy use and production methods. The greatest risks will be with those that choose to ignore these trends and try to carry on with business as usual.

U.S. Automakers Are Opposing Efforts to Reduce Greenhouse Gas Emissions

Harry Stoffer

Harry Stoffer is a reporter for Automotive News, *a magazine that provides in-depth coverage of the automotive industry.*

Automakers and dealers are mounting a full court press against states that seek to adopt California's rules aimed at reducing greenhouse gas emissions. New York, Oregon and Vermont are the targets of the latest industry lawsuits. More lawsuits may follow. At least nine states are likely to enact a version of the California regulations. The centerpiece of the litigation is a year-old federal court lawsuit that pits automaker associations and some dealers against California officials. The state adopted landmark greenhouse gas rules in 2004.

The industry calls the California rules illegal and economically ruinous. Environmental activists say the industry should be figuring out how to comply with the rules instead of battling them in court. The California rules take effect in 2006. Their provisions are scheduled to be phased in during the 2009–16 model years. The regulations mandate a 30 percent cut in emissions, primarily of carbon dioxide, a byproduct of burning fuel. The fight is the biggest regulatory challenge for the industry in a generation. Although the precise legal arguments vary from state to state, the basic issue is the same.

Not Legal, Industry Says

The industry says state limits on greenhouse gas emissions are an illegal attempt to regulate fuel economy; only the federal

Harry Stoffer, "Automakers Battle Carbon Dioxide Rules on Many Fronts," *Automotive News*, vol. 80, no. 6179, December 5, 2005, p. 4. Copyright 2005 Crain Communications, Inc. Reproduced by permission.

government has that power. State-by-state regulation would disrupt the market and boost vehicle prices by an average of $3,000, car companies and dealers say.

The [auto] industry [claims] that carbon dioxide, which is a natural part of the atmosphere, isn't a pollutant that California can regulate.

On the other side, "so many states run by people of both parties have said that we have to fight global warming, and this is a step that makes a lot of sense," says David Doniger, lawyer and climate policy director of the Natural Resources Defense Council. The council is one of several environmental groups intervening in the case on California's behalf. Doniger says the federal Clean Air Act gives California the authority to regulate "any substance" that is emitted and has harmful health effects. Such effects include climate change, he says.

The industry counters that carbon dioxide, which is a natural part of the atmosphere, isn't a pollutant that California can regulate. Many scientists say carbon dioxide is accumulating in excessive amounts, trapping heat in the atmosphere and creating potentially cataclysmic changes in climate.

The federal lawsuit against California is unlikely to be resolved soon. Court records indicate a trial is scheduled for [sometime in] 2007. The losing side is almost certain to appeal. In a small victory for the Industry in October [2005], a federal judge in California rejected a state motion to dismiss the lawsuit seeking to block the new rules. State officials said the plaintiffs had filed prematurely.

Long Court Battle

The Alliance of Automobile Manufacturers is the principal industry group fighting the California rules. Alliance Vice President Gloria Bergquist says: "We're starting down a road that could take a long time." The alliance represents the Big 3

[General Motors, DaimlerChrysler, and Ford] and six import-brand automakers. The Association of International Automobile Manufacturers, which represents 14 car companies, also is intervening in the case. The Bush administration has not entered the case, but it is trying to shore up industry arguments. Regulations that set new fuel economy standards reaffirm federal authority over the issue.

In the industry's case against New York, the alliance and some dealers say regulators did not follow proper procedures in adopting greenhouse gas rules. In the Oregon case, the alliance, some dealers and state lawmakers say Gov. Ted Kulongoski violated the state constitution. Kulongoski vetoed parts of legislation intended to prevent adoption of greenhouse gas rules. The Vermont case is a federal lawsuit similar to the lawsuit in California.

Doniger says industry executives are wasting the lead time they should use to prepare vehicles for compliance with greenhouse gas rules. Says Doniger: "We wish they would lock up their lawyers and put their engineers to work."

States and Greenhouse Gas Rules

These states have enacted, are adopting, or are considering greenhouse gas rules:

States with greenhouse gas rules:

- California

- New York

- Vermont

- Washington (contingent on Oregon)

- Maine

States close to adopting greenhouse gas rules:

- Oregon

- Massachusetts

- Connecticut

- Rhode Island

- New Jersey

States considering greenhouse gas rules:

- Pennsylvania

- North Carolina

- Arizona

- New Mexico

U.S. Companies Facing Regulatory Pressures at Home Are Moving Abroad

Sara Shipley Hiles and Marina Walker Guevara

Sara Shipley Hiles and Marina Walker Guevara are reporters for the Center for Investigative Reporting, a news organization that produces news stories for television, radio, print, and the Web.

Leslie Warden had been on a plane only once before traveling to Peru in April 2003. She didn't speak Spanish, had no college education, let alone a toxicology degree. Yet here she was, testifying in Lima's stately Legislative Palace, in a hearing room filled with legislators and their staffs, representatives from government health and mining agencies, television cameras, and reporters. She'd come to talk about the Doe Run Co., one of the world's largest lead producers, which operated a smelter in her hometown of Herculaneum, Missouri. The company now faced scrutiny over its smelter in La Oroya, a town high in the Andes Mountains where virtually every child had lead poisoning. The Peruvian Congress was considering whether to declare it a disaster zone. . . .

The story of these two towns and how they found each other illustrates an increasingly common pattern: A company faced with mounting public pressure and environmental costs in the United States expands its dirty operations abroad, where regulations are lax, labor costs low, and natural resources abundant—and where impoverished people become dependent on the jobs and charity of the very business that causes them harm. . . .

The History of Lead Pollution

The history of lead is a long and deadly one. Today, we know that exposure to lead causes anemia, high blood pressure, developmental delay, behavioral problems, decreased intelligence, and central nervous system damage. Children are the most vulnerable; no amount of lead in their bloodstreams is considered safe. But the malleable silver-gray metal has always held an allure. Ancient Egyptians laced pottery glaze with lead, and some scholars believe that its use in piping water, sweetening wine, and seasoning food contributed to the fall of Rome.

Even when the evidence of lead's harmfulness became insurmountable, the [lead] industry insisted its products were safe if used properly.

The U.S. government began phasing out leaded gasoline in 1973, after research showed that lead exposure harms the nervous system. It banned the sale of residential lead-based paint in 1978. Yet because lead remains an important component in electronics, computer monitors, and car batteries—which typically contain 21 pounds of lead—worldwide consumption has grown to more than 6 million tons a year.

Even when the evidence of lead's harmfulness became insurmountable, the industry insisted its products were safe if used properly, and it routinely suppressed data that proved their toxicity. Many companies, including Doe Run, have also made a practice of blaming the victims: children who put lead-painted toys in their mouths, or uneducated parents who live in decrepit houses. As David Rosner, a public health historian at Columbia University and an expert witness in a lawsuit against Doe Run, concludes, "It's really a pattern that develops. Shirking responsibility, denying the reality of the research, saying it wasn't their lead. So kids continue, to this day, to suffer."

The Lead Emergency in Herculaneum

Herculaneum had been polluted for decades, but public sentiment toward Doe Run began to sour in the early '90s, after an ugly labor dispute. The smelter's emissions repeatedly violated air-pollution roles, and many children were tested with high levels of lead in their blood. Some residents joined a personal injury lawsuit against the company, in the beginning of what would become an avalanche of suits against it. After the Fish and Wildlife Service found high levels of lead in fish, mice, frogs, and birds near Herculaneum, the Environmental Protection Agency [EPA] and the Missouri Department of Natural Resources issued an order in 2000 requiring Doe Run to install new pollution controls and clean up residents' yards that had lead levels exceeding EPA standards. If the smelter's emissions didn't come into compliance, the company would be forced to limit its production capacity by 20 percent.

It was the toughest enforcement action ever taken against Doe Run, but the Wardens [the business's owners] remained skeptical. Their teenage son had passed the age when children are most vulnerable to lead poisoning, but their young niece and nephew had been diagnosed with high blood-lead levels. Leslie Warden continued to scour reports, attend public meetings, and consult with environmental groups.

[A study showed that] 56 percent of the children living within a quarter mile of the [Doe Run lead] smelter had high blood-lead levels.

Finally, on an August night in 2001 [Leslie's husband] Jack Warden cornered Dave Mosby, a state environmental official. Warden insisted that Mosby sample the black dust piled thick along streets Doe Run's trucks used to haul lead to the smelter. The Wardens had long suspected the dust would test "hot."

"It was close to midnight," Mosby recalls. "But even from the streetlight, I could tell he had a real issue, because you could see the metallic luster of the dust in the street." When Mosby got the results back several days later, he was stunned to learn that the dust was 30 percent pure lead. "We knew we had an emergency situation," he says. The state health department declared Herculaneum's lead contamination "an imminent and substantial endangerment" and posted signs warning parents not to let their children play in the street.

In February 2002, state health officials released a study showing that 56 percent of the children living within a quarter mile of the smelter had high blood-lead levels. In a settlement with the state, Doe Run offered to buy 160 homes located within three-eighths of a mile of the smelter. The relocations cost the company more than $10 million, on top of the millions it spent on cleanup. . . .

The Company Moves to Peru

With the climate in Herculaneum growing increasingly tense, Renco [Doe Run's parent company] acquired a smelter in Peru. By 2005 the new facility was generating almost four times as much revenue as the Missouri smelter—and spewing 31 times as much lead into the air.

Four hours from Lima, the town of La Oroya is a labyrinth of narrow streets and one-room adobe houses located in Peru's central sierra. Years of acid rain have stained the surrounding limestone mountains black and burned them bare of vegetation. Some call the copper-colored Mantaro River that runs through the area the "dead river" because contamination has snuffed out its plant and animal life. Wrapped in fumes, Doe Run's smelter sits on the riverbank opposite the town of 33,000, dusting it with lead, arsenic, and cadmium. Sulfur in the air burns eyes and throats. In La Oroya Antigua, the neighborhood closest to the smelter, residents constantly wipe toxic dust off their furniture and windows.

An American company, Cerro de Pasco Copper Corp., built the smelter in 1922, and residents soon got used to covering their noses and mouths with handkerchiefs. As early as the '60s, lead poisoning was known to be a problem for smelter workers, though studies weren't conducted among the general population for three more decades. The Peruvian government took over the plant in 1974 and ran it for the next 23 years.

With fewer regulatory obstacles than in the United States, running a dirty [lead] smelter abroad can be far more devastating than at home.

Doe Run acquired the aging complex in 1997 for $125 million, plus another $120 million in upgrades. The facility could produce up to 152,000 tons of lead a year, plus 2.4 million pounds of silver and almost 6,000 pounds of gold. Peru had just passed its first national environmental laws, and as part of the purchase, Doe Run agreed to comply with a 10-year environmental cleanup plan. It made some improvements, such as building a disposal pit for highly toxic arsenic trioxide. According to the company, its workers' blood-lead levels dropped 30 percent, and lead and arsenic emissions from the main smokestack decreased more than a quarter over the next eight years. Yet a 2003 environmental study and government inspection records show that after Doe Run took over, the concentrations of lead, sulfur dioxide, and arsenic in La Oroya's air increased. The study suggested that the causes were a 30 percent increase in lead production and "fugitive" emissions from the plant, which specializes in processing profitable "dirty ore" loaded with contaminants.

"Doe Run had to spend millions of dollars in Herculaneum to clean up the mess they created," says Anna Cederstav, an environmental scientist with the law firm Earthjustice who has cowritten a book about La Oroya. "If they can go abroad and make a quick buck in places where they are not highly regulated, and send those profits home to pay the bills in the United States, they will absolutely do so."

Doe Run spokeswoman Barbara Shepard calls that analysis "misguided." She argues that La Oroya is better off today than it was when the Peruvian government ran the plant: Doe Run has spent more than $100 million to address environmental issues in La Oroya, and it plans to spend $100 million more in the next few years. "We are making the tough decisions alongside our community partners that will ensure sustainable development, economic growth, and improved environmental conditions," Shepard says.

Lead Poisoning in La Oroya

Like Herculaneum, La Oroya is a company town. Doe Run employs about 4,000 workers there, and those who don't work at the smelter drive taxis and wash laundry for those who do. The company operates a soup kitchen and public showers, and gives away Barbie dolls and toy robots at Christmas. The city's schools and even the police station are painted Doe Run's corporate colors, green and white, and kids wear Doe Run sweat shirts. The company says it has spent more than $6.5 million on social programs in La Oroya and the surrounding communities.

Such corporate paternalism has a long history in Peru, observes Miguel Morales, former president of Peru's National Mining Association. "Mining companies become the state, the government, the mother, the father—everything," he says. Indeed, La Oroya's mayor is a vocal supporter of Doe Run, and opposing it brings risk: The head of the Peruvian Directorate of Mining lost her job in 2005 after openly criticizing the company.

With fewer regulatory obstacles than in the United States, running a dirty smelter abroad can be far more devastating than at home. One study found that as many as 1 in every 50 people in one section of La Oroya could expect to get cancer;

the EPA's acceptable risk range is 1 in 100,000 to 1 in 1,000,000. Multiple studies, including ones by Doe Run, have found that children under seven in La Oroya Antigua have blood-lead levels about three times higher than the internationally accepted standard. A 2005 study found 44 percent of children under five in the neighborhood had mental or motor deficiencies, and nearly 10 percent of children under seven had enough lead in their blood to warrant medical treatment. "These children have been seriously damaged as a result of lead contamination," says Jorge Albinagorta, head of Peru's Office of Environmental Health. "Some have difficulties walking; others don't respond well to stimulation or their growth is stunted.". . .

Cleaning Up Doe Run's Peru Plant

Word about the problems in La Oroya traveled back to Missouri through Hunter Farrell, an American missionary who happened upon the town in 2001 and was moved by the sight of two young boys coughing violently in the streets. . . .

In August 2005, scientists from St. Louis University in Missouri arrived in La Oroya lugging boxes of dust wipes, plastic baggies, syringes, and test tubes. As boys played in a dusty plaza, one team of researchers entered a small adobe home at the end of a dirt alley. They sampled water from the spigot, examined family members, and took medical histories. . . .

For months, Doe Run had been threatening to close the smelter unless the government extended the 10-year cleanup deadline it had agreed to in 1997. . . . [In May 2006], the Peruvian government gave Doe Run a three-year extension on its cleanup. The company now must comply with stricter environmental standards and expand its health care programs. It also has to file a report whenever it sends more than $1 million stateside. To some, these requirements don't go far enough. The country's constitutional court recently ordered the health ministry to protect La Oroya residents from lead poisoning—though the ruling applies only to the government, not Doe Run. Advocates have petitioned the Inter-American Commission on Human Rights for a similar decision. Local farmers have filed a $5 billion lawsuit against Doe Run and other mining companies for damaging the Mantaro River.

But even if Doe Run completes its mandatory cleanup plan, La Oroya will remain unsafe for many years to come. According to the company's own research, many children in the town will still have blood-lead levels well above the acceptable standard. Respiratory problems will persist, and cancer risks will remain higher than U.S. standards. Residents have few ways to rid their bodies of the high levels of heavy metals confirmed by the St. Louis University study. A day-care program paid for by Doe Run has helped lower the blood-lead levels of kids with the highest readings, but by only 15 percent. More cases of severe lead poisoning have appeared in La Oroya Antigua, with one child testing at nine times the accepted standard.

Multinational Corporations Are Polluting China

Jianqiang Liu

Jianqiang Liu is a senior investigative journalist with China Southern Weekend, *one of China's most popular newspapers.*

Over the [years 2002–2005], the Chinese government . . . punished 33 multinational corporations for violating the nation's environmental laws and regulations, according to Ma Jun, director of the nongovernmental Institute of Public & Environmental Affairs. Ma's announcement in September [2005] came as a surprise to many, as the Chinese public has tended to assume that multinational companies abide more strictly by the law than some in fact do in this heavily polluted country.

World-Renowned Companies Exposed

The exposed companies include subsidiaries of world-renowned corporations such as American Standard, Panasonic, Pepsi, Nestlé, and 3M. They were punished mainly for discharges of substandard waste water and for unauthorized construction activities that occurred in the absence of proper environmental impact assessments.

When researchers at Ma's institute began building a database to map China's water pollution [in 2006], they used data from the websites of various Chinese environmental protection authorities. During the process, they came across a list of multinational corporations that had been cited for environmentally harmful activities for the years 2004–06.

Ma, who once worked as an environmental consultant for multinationals in China, was shocked by the discovery. "Those enterprises have been talking about corporate responsibility, yet they could not even abide by the law," he says. "On the one hand, multinational corporations have not kept their environmental promise with respect to a global uniform standard; on the other hand, the implementation power of environmental laws and regulations in China is very weak."

Companies are more willing to invest in public relations than in actually cleaning up the manufacturing process.

Mr. Zhao, an authority with the Jilin Provincial Environmental Protection Bureau agrees that "multinational corporations have relaxed their environmental standards in China." And according to Lo Sze Ping, campaign director of Greenpeace China, the "words" of multinationals are often better than their deeds. To address their wrongdoings, companies are more willing to invest in public relations than in actually cleaning up the manufacturing process, he says.

A Lack of Oversight of Multinationals

What concerns environmentalists more, however, is the weak governmental and legal oversight of multinational corporations. Lo observes that as local governments seek to attract foreign investment, their affiliated environmental protection bureaus dare not take strict measures to address pollution by multinational corporations. He also believes that since multinational corporations typically perform better than domestic enterprises environmentally, the sub-par activities of foreign companies won't attract the attention of the country's top environmental authority, the State Environmental Protection Administration. This leaves a void in supervision.

But Lo also points out that domestic enterprises are more likely than multinationals to lack the capacity to meet environmental protection standards, while for the foreign firms it is more often a matter of willingness to address such problems. "Multinationals should be the 'lead goat' of their industries," he says.

William Valentino, general manager for corporate communications for Bayer Corporation and the chair of the Corporate Social Responsibility Working Group of the European Chamber of Commerce in China, agrees that the poor environmental performance of domestic enterprises should not be used as an excuse for multinationals. "Talk about home electronic appliances, Chinese people will think of Sony; talk about soft drinks, they will think of Coca-Cola. As an international enterprise trusted by the Chinese people, one is obliged to bear more responsibilities," Valentino says.

Corporations Are Working with Environmentalists and Going Green

Katherine Mangu-Ward

Katherine Mangu-Ward is an associate editor of Reason, *an award-winning monthly magazine with both a print and an online edition that espouses libertarian principles.*

Ask Bob Langert about the Environmental Protection Agency (EPA), and he starts to chuckle. "When we meet the regulators, it's kind of nice," says the senior director for social responsibility at the McDonald's Corporation. "We just got an award from the EPA. When we see the regulators, we always hope it's because they're giving us an award."

Such coziness between big business and big government might make readers nervous—but it's not what you think. McDonald's won this year's Climate Protection Award by cooperating with Greenpeace to build a prototype McDonald's restaurant with greener refrigerant technologies, which reduce problematic emissions from cooling units and cut energy costs by 17 percent. Cooperation between corporations and greens was done right, and everybody won. . . .

The Turn Toward Voluntary Environmental Programs

The idea of the rich corporate villain gleefully dirtying Mother Earth is powerful and appealing. Children of the 1980s encountered this supervillain in comics, movies, public aware-

Katherine Mangu-Ward, "The Age of Corporate Environmentalism: Surprise—Big Business Has Learned that It's Pretty Easy Being Green," *Reason*, February 2006. www.reason.com/news/show/36208.html. Copyright 2006 by Reason Foundation, 3415 S. Sepulveda Blvd., Suite 400, Los Angeles, CA 90034. www.reason.com. Reproduced by permission.

ness videos, and science textbooks. Times were good for mandatory recycling, for mandatory emissions reductions, for anything mandatory aimed at restraining corporate polluters.

To ward off excessive regulation, help the bottom line, and get brownie points at the same time, companies started playing nice with environmental groups.

But in the late '90s, something peculiar started happening. The men in suits were still middle-aged, round, and white. They were still just as concerned with profit and golf. Very few of them sported tie-dyed attire, aside from the occasional whimsical Jerry Garcia tie. But the men in suits started caring. Or at least acting like they cared. Which, if you ask a spotted owl, is the same thing. So environmental activists across the nation bought their own ties and started dealing with corporation as almost-equal partners in planet saving. Businesses in turn learned that it's pretty easy being green.

"What's hot right now are voluntary environmental programs," says Jorge Rivera, assistant professor at the George Washington University business school. Mandatory environmentalism is "effective, but expensive," Rivera says, and it often produces nothing but "greenwashing," where companies satisfy the letter of the law as quickly and as cheaply as they can rather than making a serious effort to innovate. (In some cases, this actually means an increase in environmental damage, as when harmful emissions are converted to less-regulated but more harmful forms.) And since "a lot of the big, obvious stuff has already been done," Rivera notes, it isn't really effective to mandate uniform change to bring about marginal gains. So to ward off excessive regulation, help the bottom line, and get brownie points at the same time, companies started playing nice with environmental groups.

A Lack of Government Environmentalism

Meanwhile, by the end of 2000, Greenpeace, Environmental Defense, et al. were realizing that the government wasn't a reliable ally anymore. Corporations started to look awfully appealing when the alternative was George W. Bush. Gwen Ruta, director of corporate partnerships at Environmental Defense, claims private initiatives are "the wave of the future," in part because "we're in a rather uncertain regulatory period. How aggressive will the government be in the next few years in creating regulations?

"We don't know. And so we're looking to partner with companies to go beyond regulations." Unlike in the '80s, when an adversarial relationship with government simply sparked more grassroots enthusiasm, Bush's unwillingness to increase environmental regulation seemed contagious. The widespread excitement about saving the planet was spent, perhaps because "a lot of the big obvious stuff" *had* already been done. And green activists weren't generating headlines the way they used to. The radicals broke away, with groups like Friends of the Earth and the Earth Liberation Front determined to continue in a pure anti-corporate vein, but well-established environmental groups decided their best option was to play nice.

Environmental groups are (mostly) thrilled to have made so much progress . . . but are still understandably wary of the corporations' motives.

As the environmental bureaucracy became an emasculated dispenser of the occasional award, many greens decided that they had no choice but to suck it up and try to figure out how to work with men who consider bowties a daring fashion statement. Ruta works with companies to help them "keep moving forward, aside from government regulation." Her project has brokered deals with McDonald's, Starbucks, UPS, Bristol-Myers Squibb, and Federal Express.

Corporate Motives

Environmental groups are (mostly) thrilled to have made so much progress—FedEx drivers in San Francisco use hybrid delivery trucks, Starbucks uses fewer disposable cups—but are still understandably wary of the corporations' motives. Perhaps you too suspect that companies are making nice with greens only for the good P.R. And perhaps you suspect that they only make changes when there's a profit to be made. If so, you are almost completely right.

But there are better and worse ways to strike the balance between the demands of shareholders and the demands of Greenpeace. For an example of a company apparently trying to single-handedly save the planet through expensive public relations alone, one needn't look farther than the corporate darling of serious environmentalists and greenish consumers alike: BP. BP is first among many companies that have opted to do their environmental penance in the glare of the spotlight. British Petroleum (recently rechristened BP, following KFC's model in removing unsavory words from its brand name) has been much ballyhooed for its commitment to the environment. Most of the ballyhooing is being done by BP itself.

Home Depot ... decided to use its power in the lumber market to do some good—after a little gentle prodding from the Rainforest Action Network.

A gas and oil company with $225 billion in revenue, BP is part of an industry that will keep environmental advocacy groups in business for as long at it exists. Yet these days BP is styling itself "Beyond Petroleum" and declaring that it's "thinking outside the barrel." BP's Environmental Team has crafted an elaborate advertising campaign and rebranding effort, recently expanded to the Web. Its goal: to convince the world that a company that sucks dead dinosaurs out of the earth, turns them into gasoline, and delivers that gas to SUVs can also be environmentally friendly enough to use a green and yellow sunburst (or is it a flower?) as its logo.

On the company's Web site, casual visitors can select from the following tabs: "About BP," "Environment and Society," and "Products and Services." In that order. Never mind that BP's spending on green projects constitutes less than half of 1 percent of its revenue. It publicly supports stricter pollution regulations and the Kyoto Protocols, the international agreement calling for reductions in greenhouse gas emissions, and gives money to groups that lobby for both. BP is selling itself as the anti-ExxonMobil.

ExxonMobil has long been a favorite target of environmental activists, especially since the tanker *Exxon Valdez* sank off the coast of Alaska in 1989, covering all those adorable Arctic animals in oil. Unlike BP, the company publicly opposes the Kyoto Protocols and has done so for years. That isn't its biggest problem, though. According to Robert L. Bradley Jr., president of the Houston-based Institute for Energy Research, one major reason environmentalists go after ExxonMobil is the company's history of funding free market groups such as the Competitive Enterprise Institute and the Heartland Institute (and Bradley's own organization).

Ironically, Exxon is also one of the biggest investors in clean technology. Their recent safety record is also significantly better than BP's. Says George Washington's Rivera, "The surprising thing about Exxon is that their facilities are run very well." Better, in fact, than BP's: After a March [2005] explosion at a BP plant in Texas City [Texas] that killed 15 people and injured 170, the EPA and other agencies concluded that the deaths were preventable and that they were primarily the result of carelessness by BP management. The *Houston Chronicle* editorialized that "BP's carefully nourished image as an environmentally sensitive, innovative company is at odds with its history, particularly in the Houston area."

Picturesque Causes

But while Exxon spends its money on free market think tanks, BP has chosen more picturesque causes. Delve into its Web site and you'll find that BP is funding the Conservation Programme, which, among other things, sends students to Colombia to study "a species of parrot threatened with extinction." After an "intensive search across the Andes for several of Colombia's threatened parrot species" in 2002, "the team was the first to discover nests of the azure-winged parrot, the rusty-faced parrot and other threatened bird species." If the rusty-faced parrot and his fine feathered friends aren't your thing, there's always the Iberian lynx. BP is "trying to involve our customers in the campaign to save the species by awarding them loyalty points that can be used to purchase guided tours through the lynx preserve or other promotional materials including T-shirts and calendars." It is also "mobilizing Malaysians to take action on climate change." One might be forgiven for wondering how BP is managing to take in hundreds of billions in oil and gas revenue, apparently in its spare time.

By exceeding expectations a little—and then making a big deal out of it—BP avoids getting singled out as a bogeyman. If environmental groups are going to choose someone to target, why not encourage them to choose your competitor? And if shareholders question the money spent "mobilizing Malaysians," they'll be glad enough when the next protest against the oil industry is held outside Exxon's headquarters instead of BP's.

The trouble is, there will always be someone who wants you to do more. Bradley has found allies against BP in an unlikely place: the far left. "They are very critical of BP because they know that 99.5 percent of their capital expenditures are related to fossil fuels, and a small increment is related to solar," he reports. "ExxonMobil is still the bad guy, but we are getting increasingly frustrated with BP and Shell, which talk about climate change but put their money into" oil and gas, Roger Higman, an activist at Friends of the Earth, told *The Guardian* in 2003. "We are not going to be cozy with them because they are doing bad things."

In 2005 Home Depot sold more than $400 million in [certified] wood. . . . Its does not buy old-growth timber or wood from . . . rainforests.

The money BP spends to "partner" with environmental groups might look, from a certain angle, like a bribe to prevent protests. But the bribery goes both ways. Corporations are learning to respond to what Tom Murray of Environmental Defense says are "carrots in a system which is, in many ways, all sticks." For the moment, the marriage of convenience between BP and environmental activists remains intact and fairly functional. But both sides recognize that they have struck a delicate balance.

Greening Home Depot

Home Depot offers another, perhaps more sustainable model of green-corporate cooperation. It decided to use its power in the lumber market to do some good—after a little gentle prodding from the Rainforest Action Network. Ron Jarvis, now Home Depot's vice president of merchandising for lumber products, enjoys recounting the tizzy his career trajectory caused in environmental circles. In 1999 Jarvis' bosses asked him to leave his position as a regional merchandise manager and come to their Atlanta headquarters to serve as the environmental global product manager. A "shock wave went through some of the environmental groups," he says. They were aghast that "Home Depot had just taken one of their lumber guys and put [him] over the environment."

Politically speaking, the late '90s had been rough years for the company. The Rainforest Action Network (RAN) had targeted it for selling wood from illegally cut rainforests and old-growth forests. And when RAN targets you, expect more than a letter writing campaign. On May 25, 1999, the group announced a day of "ethical shoplifting" and encouraged its members to "borrow" timber from Home Depots across the country, which they later handed over to the FBI. A guy in a black bear costume affixed himself to one store's rafters and hollered through a bullhorn about Home Depot's failings. It wasn't clear that Home Depot, a national chain frequented by suburban men primarily interested in low prices and the horsepower available in competing models of riding lawnmowers, would have the will or the energy to transform itself.

In 2005 Home Depot sold more than $400 million in wood certified by the Forest Stewardship Council. It does not buy old-growth timber or wood from recently cleared rainforests. Its Web site boasts that "typical Team Depot activities include conservation projects, beautification efforts, and cleanups."...

Four-hundred million dollars seems like a lot of wood, and Home Depot is the largest lumber buyer in the world. But its purchases account for only about 1 percent of the trees cut down worldwide. Still, says Jarvis, who has the authority to sever logging contracts with any supplier whose practices harm endangered forests or otherwise injure the environment, "Does that mean that we turn our back and walk away and say that we do not have a social responsibility, that the impact's not great enough? No."

Actually, as Jarvis recently reminded an audience at the Companies for Corporate Responsibility investor conference, Home Depot has been buying certified wood since 1994. The problem, it discovered, was that the supply of certified wood wasn't adequate; people still bought the cheaper, uncertified stuff if given the choice. After RAN's campaign grew more intense, Home Depot decided to use its market power to reduce the price of certified wood by selling it exclusively. The will, Jarvis says, was there all along. The company just needed a little reassurance that customers who wouldn't pay extra from conscience alone would still buy at Home Depot when asked to fork over a few more cents per two-by-four.

After creating a cruelty-to-endangered-species-and-old-tree-free lumber department, Jarvis and his team expanded their efforts to include the wood involved in manufactured products in other departments. To call Jarvis an environmentalist is just as inaccurate as calling him a "lumber guy." He doesn't fit the stereotype of either. The problem he says, is that environmentalists and their corporate counterparts "couldn't speak the same language for years."

Top U.S. Companies
Are Reducing
Global-Warming Emissions

Jessica Seid

Jessica Seid is a staff writer for CNN/Money, *a business and financial magazine.*

Government caps on the emission of global-warming gases could cost big bucks for companies forced to comply with the rules. But has the business world come to terms with the financial implications of climate change? And though the costs could be high for some, other companies seem much better positioned. A few may even be poised to benefit. "Some firms have already moved ahead," said David Victor, director of the Program on Energy and Sustainable Development at Stanford University.

Innovest Strategic Value Advisors, an investment research firm specializing in analyzing companies' performance on environmental issues, identified a "top 100" list of companies that are most open to environmental regulations. For instance, General Electric has set its sights on the growing wind power market and may see a windfall from clean energy technologies. The company's financial arm also recently announced an initiative to provide financial solutions to the growing number of companies focused on clean energy and related technologies.

Cummins Inc. has sold thousands of compressed natural gas bus engines to Beijing, which has the world's largest bus fleet operating on clean energy. Cummins has also established a business relationship in India to introduce natural gas engines there, the company said in a statement.

BP, owner of one of the world's largest solar power businesses, is introducing lower-emissions fuels at its retail outlets. "We'll continue to shift the balance of our business in favor of lower carbon energy sources and in particular natural gas," Group Chief Executive John Browne said in a statement.

Now that a United Nations plan to limit emissions of greenhouse gases has taken effect, companies in participating countries face more stringent regulation.

The No. 1 aluminum producer, Alcoa, is poised to benefit from the auto industry's adoption of aluminum to create fuel-efficient vehicles with better strength-to-weight ratios that produce lower emissions. Aluminum's use in vehicles is rapidly increasing due to a heightened need for fuel efficient, environmentally friendly vehicles, according to the Aluminum Association.

Toyota Motors' investment in environmental technology for the auto industry will also position the automaker well to face new climate change policies. Hybrids are already in high demand, but production levels have been relatively small. Still, Toyota's hybrid Prius was the fastest selling car in the U.S. [in 2004].

"If automobile efficiency gets serious then hybrid cars may not be the best choice," Victor warns. Companies that produce new generation diesel engines, for example, may turn out to be the big winners. "With advanced fuels there are next-to-no traditional air pollutants, making diesel engines amazingly efficient," according to Victor. With the manifestation of legitimate and credible emissions rules, some firms with access to new technologies may emerge relatively quickly. And with research increasingly indicating a demand for climate change policy, it is likely that more companies will address their own preparedness.

The U.S. emits approximately 25 percent of the world's greenhouse gases, ... but is not a participant in the Kyoto Protocol, arguing it is too costly.

In the Hot House

Concerns that the greenhouse effect poses a serious threat to the global environment are not new. Now that a United Nations plan to limit emissions of greenhouse gases has taken effect, companies in participating countries face more stringent regulation. The Kyoto Protocol was enacted Feb. 16 [2005] and requires 38 of the world's industrialized nations—including Canada, Japan, Russia and all of the European Union—to reduce greenhouse gas emissions 5 percent below 1990 levels by 2012.

The U.S. emits approximately 25 percent of the world's greenhouse gases, according to the Energy Information Administration, but is not a participant in the Kyoto Protocol, arguing it is too costly. The State Department said the White House is committed to cutting greenhouse gas emissions and announced it will spend nearly $5.8 billion on research and programs addressing climate change.

Climate change policy in response to the greenhouse effect aims to limit emissions of certain gases, including carbon dioxide, methane, nitrous oxide, water vapor and chlorofluorocarbons, that trap the sun's heat in the Earth's atmosphere and are believed to raise global temperatures and disrupt weather patterns. According to the United Nations Intergovernmental Panel on Climate Change (IPCC), deforestation and the burning of fossil fuels have increased the amount of greenhouse gases in the atmosphere and caused rising temperatures. In addition, all carbon dioxide emissions, some natural and some caused by burning of fossil fuels, will continue to heighten the greenhouse effect.

Some critics of the IPCC report say the temperature changes from the 20th century are within the bounds of normal variability. Others cite faulty research data, and believe surface temperatures alone do not provide the best gauge of climate change.

In an interview with the BBC, James L. Connaughton, chairman of the United States Council on Environmental Quality, said that the science was still contested. "We are still working on the issue of causation, the extent to which humans are a factor," he said.

Success Will Come to Companies That Contribute to a Sustainable Environment

World Business Council for Sustainable Development

The World Business Council for Sustainable Development (WBCSD) is a coalition of more than 180 international companies united by a shared commitment to sustainable development through economic growth, ecological balance, and social progress.

[The World Business Council for Sustainable Development believes] that the fundamental purpose of business is to provide continually improving goods and services for increasing numbers of people at prices that they can afford. We believe that this statement of our purpose unites the interests of business and society at the deepest level. It makes clear that we prosper by helping society to prosper, by innovating to create new goods and services and by reaching out to new customers.

A Model for Sustainable Development

We believe that the leading global companies of 2020 will be those that provide goods and services and reach new customers in ways that address the world's major challenges—including poverty, climate change, resource depletion, globalization, and demographic shifts.

If action to address such issues is to be substantial and sustainable, it must also be profitable. Our major contribution to society will therefore come through our core business, rather than through our philanthropic programs. We see shareholder value as a measure of how successfully we deliver value to society, rather than as an end in itself.

In aligning our interests with the needs of society, we will follow a model based on our own experience and analysis of successful business strategies:

- We will develop an understanding of how global issues such as poverty, the environment, demographic change, and globalization affect our individual companies and sectors.

- We will use our understanding of the significance of these signals to search for business opportunities that help to address them.

- We will develop our core business strategies to align them with the opportunities that we have identified.

- We will incorporate long-term measures into our definition of success, targeting profitability that is sustainable, supported by a positive record in social, environmental, and employment areas. . . .

Any successful company will both create shareholder value and operate responsibly. In fact these amount to the same thing.

Business Does Good by Doing Business

Any successful company will both create shareholder value and operate responsibly. In fact these amount to the same thing. Most companies benefit society simply by doing business. We meet customers' needs for goods and services. We create jobs. We pay wages and salaries. We provide for employees and families through pensions and health plans. We innovate to create products that contribute to human progress. We pay taxes that fund public services and infrastructure. We create work for millions of suppliers, many of them small- and medium-sized companies. Our search for competitive advantage leads to efficiency, and thus to reduced consumption of resources, less pollution, and higher quality products.

The purpose of any business that seeks to be sustainable has to be more than generating short-term shareholder value. Simply by adding the word *long-term* to *shareholder value*, we embrace everything necessary for the survival and success of the company. This includes building trust among communities and maintaining a healthy environment in which to do business.

All of these benefits are created in the normal course of responding to market signals.

A company that acts to protect the environment is helping to preserve the natural capital upon which its operations depend.

Smart Businesses Pick Up Societal Signals

Progressive businesses are now widening their horizons as they look for opportunities and are gaining competitive advantage by responding to societal signals as well as market signals. For example, a company that acts to promote human welfare is helping to build its future market and workforce. A company that acts to protect the environment is helping to preserve the natural capital upon which its operations depend and possibly gaining early-mover advantage in the more highly-regulated markets of the future. Such companies realize that ignoring these issues means—at best—missing early indicators of future profitabilty and—at worst—risking the company's market valuation and reputation.

The products are the purpose—the profits are the prize. In responding to societal signals, companies are now looking more widely and imaginatively at the fundamental purpose of providing continually improving goods and services to increasing numbers of customers at prices they can afford. They are improving their products in ways that serve societal ends, and they are increasing customer numbers by reaching out to new markets in developing and emerging economies.

In this view of the role of business, shareholder value is seen as the measure of success in fulfilling the more fundamental purpose of providing improving goods and services that today's and tomorrow's consumers want.

As a result of responding to societal signals, many companies are now active in areas often considered the domain of governments; providing basic goods such as health, education, and pensions; advocating a framework to tackle climate change; or addressing poverty through corporate strategy. . . .

If the whole world's population were to enjoy a lifestyle similar to that of the industrialized countries today, it would require the resources of 5.5 planet Earths.

Environmental Challenges

Human activity over the past 50 years has changed the world's environment more extensively than ever before, largely to meet growing demands for food, fuel, fresh water, timber, and fiber. The use of natural resources has advanced human development, but at a growing environmental cost. The UN Development Programme has estimated that if the whole world's population were to enjoy a lifestyle similar to that of the industrialized countries today, it would require the resources of 5.5 planet Earths.

The 2005 report of the international Millennium Ecosystem Assessment (MEA) group, involving 1,360 experts worldwide, revealed dramatic deterioration in ecosystem services. These include the provision of resources such as fuel and food, processes such as climate regulation, and the aesthetic and recreational values of nature. The MEA found that two-thirds of these services were being degraded or used unsustainably, and described global warming as the change with the greatest potential to alter the natural infrastructure of Earth.

Many of the world's natural resources are not owned by anyone or assigned a value. They represent common goods, and failure to halt their depletion is sometimes referred to as "the tragedy of the global commons."

We believe it is imperative to reverse this trend and operate within the carrying capacity of the earth. Our challenge is to find opportunity in doing so. Encouragingly, this is an area in which business is beginning to find ways to turn responsibility into opportunity. We now must do it on a scale that has an impact at the global level.

Sustainable Consumption and Supply

Many companies are finding opportunities in encouraging customers to act in a more sustainable way. For example, in Canada, BC Hydro has a Power Smart program that provides financial incentives to customers who replace existing inefficient products with energy-efficient technologies. Heineken N.V. is using its beer bottles to promote a website which includes responsible consumption guidelines.

The market of consumers willing to pay a premium for products that have environmental benefits but cost more to produce, such as ultra low-sulfur fuels, is small and growing slowly. However, when the environmental benefits are accompanied by increased quality or performance, the market is likely to grow much more rapidly.

Some companies are now looking to gain early mover advantage in a more sustainable future global economy.

In cases where no regulation exists, businesses have worked with others to create global standards that lift expectations and raise the bar for industry. Examples include the Marine Stewardship Council, the Forest Stewardship Council, and

WBCSD sector projects such as the Cement Sustainability Initiative, which sets best practice with its key performance indicators.

Many companies are now working to ensure their supplies come from sustainable sources. This can create a dilemma in winning customers' support. Unilever, which markets Birds Eye frozen foods, has a target of sourcing all fish supplies from sustainable fisheries. It helped to establish the now independent Marine Stewardship Council, whose logo on a fish product indicates that the fish it contains comes from sustainable fisheries. In the UK, Unilever is limiting the use of cod, which is severely over-fished in some areas, and helping consumers understand the reasons for introducing sustainably sourced New Zealand hoki instead.

Benefits of Innovation

Companies that innovate to create cleaner technologies benefit when governments devise policies that reward progress and penalize pollution. Such benefits were gained by companies that invested to find alternatives to ozone-depleting CFCs [chlorofluorocarbons].

Some companies are now looking to gain early mover advantage in a more sustainable future global economy. As Goldman Sachs noted in its 2005 report *Sustainable Investing in the Energy Sector*. "The companies that have potential for creating significant value are those that have the most strategic options available to embrace a low-carbon world." For example, some energy companies, including BP, Shell, Statoil, ChevronTexaco, Norsk Hydro, ENI, EnCana, and Suncor Energy, are working to bring down the costs and assure the safety of technologies to capture and store carbon dioxide [CO_2], keeping it out of the atmosphere.

Monetizing Resources

Natural resources are estimated to have a value almost twice that of society's economic activities, and there is a growing trend to treat them as assets rather than free common goods. Governments are developing market mechanisms for such assets, including CO_2 emissions credits, sustainable agriculture products, and improved water pricing schemes. Companies such as Shell and BP have used internal mechanisms for emissions trading that have positioned them well in advance of mandatory initiatives such as the EU [European Union] Emissions Trading Scheme.

At the global level, where such mechanisms are more difficult to implement, one initiative under the Kyoto Treaty has been the Clean Development Mechanism (CDM), which enables states to gain credit for emissions reduction projects carried out in other countries. If practical challenges can be overcome, the CDM system could encourage transfers of resources and technology between developed and developing countries.

Policy Engagement

Where companies have products or technologies that benefit the environment but that require supportive policies to be competitive at scale, they often become public advocates for reform. Some companies advocate policies that will raise environmental standards and provide markets for cleaner technologies. Some national and state governments—for example, Japan, Germany and California—have demonstrated the progress that can be made in deploying technologies such as solar energy when effective government support is in place.

A common theme in many of these environmental experiences is the relationship of mandatory to voluntary action. In some cases regulation has prompted companies to innovate—for example, the imposition of sulfur emission limits on fuel in North America and Europe. In other cases, regulation has not been in place but companies have acted voluntarily. For example, the Panama Canal Authority is providing land deeds and loans to farmers who protect the water resources needed by the canal, effectively assigning value to watershed management. . . .

Business will continue to provide goods and services that people need, but the extent to which we simultaneously deal with the major global issues of the next few decades depends on our success in achieving clarity and consensus about our purpose and role.

Are U.S. Pollution Regulations Effective?

Chapter Preface

Superfund is the name of a U.S. government program begun in 1980 to clean up hazardous waste sites in America. In many of these locations, the soil or groundwater had been polluted with heavy metals such as arsenic, cadmium, chromium, lead, mercury, and zinc; pesticides such as DDT; and other substances that are highly toxic to humans, animals, and plant life.

Superfund was established by the Comprehensive Environmental Response, Compensation, and Liability Act (CERCLA), and initially funded with $1.8 billion in federal funds obtained from taxes imposed on major oil and chemical companies, which were considered responsible for many of the toxic sites. In 1986 more funds were appropriated, creating a total Superfund budget of $8.5 billion. The principle behind Superfund is that the polluter should pay for environmental cleanup. Under CERCLA, therefore, the U.S. Environmental Protection Agency (EPA) is authorized to identify hazardous waste sites, find the companies or individuals responsible for creating the site, and require those parties to cover the costs of cleaning up the sites. The Superfund monies are used in cases where the responsible parties cannot be identified or have declared bankruptcy.

Superfund was enacted largely as a result of the publicity surrounding Love Canal, a neighborhood in Niagara Falls, New York, that became famous in the 1970s as a toxic waste site. A landfill in this location was used by a chemical company for disposal of toxic wastes, and people living in nearby residential neighborhoods began to notice an increase in strange odors, birth defects, and high rates of cancer and other illnesses. Initially, both the company and the city denied any responsibility, but after a federal investigation, President Jimmy Carter declared a state of emergency, and more than

800 families were relocated by the government. CERCLA was passed in the wake of this disaster.

In the years following the creation of Superfund, the EPA identified about 1,600 hazardous waste sites that were deemed to be the most serious. By 2000, the EPA had completed cleanup at more than 750 of these sites, and some sites were cleaned up voluntarily, but much work remained. A 2003 EPA report found that hazardous chemicals dangerous to human health remained at more than 149 Superfund sites, and more than 225 sites continued to pollute groundwater.

Because of a 1995 decision by the U.S. Congress not to re-new the taxes on oil and chemical companies that originally funded Superfund, however, cleanup responsibility was re-moved from polluting companies just as the cost of cleanups was rising. Superfund cleanups cost approximately $300 mil-lion in 1995, but these costs jumped to around a billion dol-lars per year by the turn of the new millennium. In September 2003, Superfund used the last of the $8.5 billion raised from polluters, shifting the burden of cleanup costs completely to American taxpayers. The lack of corporate funding and rising costs have dramatically slowed the Superfund efforts. Between 1997 and 2000, the EPA cleaned up approximately 87 toxic waste sites each year, but that number dropped to 47 in 2001, 42 in 2002, and has averaged about 40 a year since then. In 2004 more than 46 sites were not funded or received inad-equate funds for clearing toxic wastes.

The danger of not cleaning up these sites was dramatically revealed in 2005 when Hurricane Katrina hit the New Orleans area, which contained several hazardous waste sites. One of the most polluted sites, for example, was the Agriculture Street Landfill, which contained about a century's worth of munici-pal garbage and industrial wastes. Before the storm, this area was so heavily polluted with lead, arsenic, dioxin, and carcino-genic hydrocarbons, as well as the now-banned pesticide DDT, that it periodically developed underground fires—earning it the nickname "Dante's Inferno." Katrina unleashed these contaminants throughout the region. As former vice president and environmentalist Al Gore said in a September 2005 speech, "When the Superfund sites aren't cleaned up, we get a toxic gumbo in a flood."

Environmental advocates have pushed for Congress and the president to reinstate the polluter tax on corporations to fund future Superfund waste efforts, but this has been opposed for years by a Republican-controlled Congress and President George W. Bush. Superfund supporters say that returning to a polluter-pays principle is the only way to fully fund the program and finish the job of cleaning up the country's toxic waste dumps. Critics of Superfund, however, argue that the program should be abandoned completely. They claim that much of the funding goes to pay lawyers, consultants, and investigators because the EPA process is one that involves suing polluting companies. In addition, they say the law inhibits urban renewal because investors do not want to develop areas that may result in toxic waste liability. Most observers believe that the program will continue in some form, but no one is certain how effective it will be.

The Superfund law is only one of several laws that regulate environmental pollution in America. The EPA also enforces air and water pollution regulations under the Clean Air Act and the Clean Water Act and seeks to comply with U.S. treaty commitments to phase out chemicals that are damaging to Earth's ozone layer, which protects those on the planet's surface from ultraviolet radiation. The viewpoints in this chapter debate some of the current issues relating to the U.S. government's pollution regulations.

The George W. Bush Administration Has Gutted Environmental Standards

Eric Schaeffer

Eric Schaeffer is director of the Environmental Integrity Project at the Rockefeller Family Fund, a philanthropy located in New York City.

Just after the 2000 election, ... my colleagues at the Environmental Protection Agency [EPA] and Justice Department celebrated a dramatic victory of their own. Two of the country's largest utilities had just agreed to cut pollution from their old, coal-fired power plants by two-thirds, or more than half a million tons a year. As director of the EPA's Office of Regulatory Enforcement since 1997, I helped to bring lawsuits against some of the nation's largest electric utilities. The government charged these companies with violating the Clean Air Act by expanding their coal-fired electric plants without controlling emissions such as nitrogen oxide and sulfur dioxide—noxious gases that cause smog, asthma, lung cancer, and premature death. The postelection settlement with Cinergy and Dominion was a landmark, pressuring other companies to follow suit and clean up their act as well.

Unfortunately, Washington's energy lobbyists understood this dynamic all too clearly. And when President [George W.] Bush assumed office [in January 2001], they wasted little time blocking this new momentum toward cleaner air by persuading the administration that the problem wasn't the polluters, but our anti-pollution laws. It wasn't a hard sell. The Bush administration quickly set about weakening the Clean Air Act,

Eric Schaeffer, "Clearing the Air: Why I Quit Bush's EPA," *Washington Monthly*, July-August 2002. www.washingtonmonthly.com/features/2001/0207.schaeffer.html. Copyright 2002 by Washington Monthly Publishing, LLC, 733 15th St. NW, Suite 520, Washington, DC 20005. (202) 393-5155. www.washingtonmonthly.com. Reproduced by permission.

stoking public fears of energy shortages and blackouts as a rationale for leniency (even though 2001 was a record year for power plant expansion). White House staff and the Energy Department, working closely with lobbyists for the same companies we had sued, directed EPA to expand loopholes that allow 40- or 50-year-old power plants to continue pumping out 12 million tons of sulfur dioxide a year, without implementing modern pollution controls. What's more, in March [2001], EPA Administrator Christine Whitman shocked everyone by publicly suggesting that companies hold off on settlements pending the outcome of litigation. Not surprisingly, Cinergy and Dominion backed out of their agreements and refused to sign consent decrees. (The administration [then] rolled out a series of "reforms" making it so easy for these big plants to avoid pollution controls that they might as well have been written by defendants' lawyers.) [Years] later, nothing has improved, and the opportunity for cleaner air that once seemed so close has been lost—the other companies, once on the path to settlement, have drifted away from the negotiating table.

The Bush Assault on Environmental Laws

In a matter of weeks, the Bush administration was able to undo the environmental progress we had worked years to secure. Millions of tons of unnecessary pollution continue to pour from these power plants each year as a result. Adding insult to injury, the White House sought to slash the EPA's enforcement budget, making it harder for us to pursue cases we'd already launched against other polluters that had run afoul of the law, from auto manufacturers to refineries, large industrial hog feedlots, and paper companies. It became clear that Bush had little regard for the environment—and even less for enforcing the laws that protect it. So [in Spring 2001], after 12 years at the agency, I resigned, stating my reasons in a very public letter to Administrator Whitman.

Enforcing environmental laws has never been easy. Even in the [Bill] Clinton administration [1993–2001] there were bureaucratic turf battles, truculent congressmen, and relentless industry lobbyists to contend with. But hard work yielded progress; the job was sometimes a headache, but I never doubted that we were having a positive effect. Under Bush, the balance has shifted, to a degree few outside the bureaucracy may realize.

Behind the scenes, . . . the [Bush] administration and its allies in Congress are crippling the EPA's ability to enforce laws and regulations already on the books.

The administration's most obvious assaults on the environment have drawn fire. The press and environmental groups attacked EPA rule changes that allow coal-mining companies to dump waste in valleys and streams, and when the EPA [in 2001] overturned Clinton-era regulations to reduce arsenic in drinking water, the public reaction was so intensely negative that Whitman eventually backed off. But these public efforts to roll back regulations are only half the story. Behind the scenes, in complicated ways that attract less media attention (and therefore may be politically safer), the administration and its allies in Congress are crippling the EPA's ability to enforce laws and regulations already on the books. As a result, some of the worst pollution continues unchecked. . . .

The Bush Strategy

The first step [by Bush] was to appoint as EPA administrator Christine Whitman, who provides a moderate face, but already had a reputation for gutting anti-pollution enforcement programs while she was governor of New Jersey. Another was to leave the enforcement program rudderless: 18 months into his [first] term, Bush ha[d] not yet filled the top EPA enforcement job. Leaving the job unfilled not only deprive[d] the staff of leadership, but also rob[bed] the administration's critics of an actual person to blame for poor performance. Bush political appointees in the White House and EPA quickly took up the many other ways of thwarting enforcement without drawing attention. Here are a few of their tricks:

Shrink the police force. Environmental law, just like any other, is a dead letter if not enforced. The Bush administration's first step was weakening the government's ability to uncover violations of important requirements like tailpipe emission standards. Each year, about 25 million tons of smog-causing nitrogen oxide is released into the air, about half of it from cars, diesel trucks, and construction equipment. For several years, the diesel engines of large long-haul trucks have been required to meet emission standards with catalytic converters that clean exhaust gases. But manufacturers realized that they could beat the system by developing catalytic converters that would run properly during EPA tests, but whose pollution controls could be turned off on the highway. In November 1998, EPA settled with nine diesel engine manufacturers—practically the entire industry—forcing the companies to spend about $1 billion to phase out these illegal engines. It was a textbook example of how enforcement is supposed to work: The settlements will eliminate about 1.3 million tons of illegal emissions a year, or about 10 percent of the total nitrogen oxide pollution from mobile sources. But winning a settlement like that takes thousands of hours of staff time, and Bush's Office of Management and Budget knows it. Cutting the enforcement budget by 13 percent, as President Bush proposed, would hobble the EPA's ability to uncover and stop such malfeasance.

Divide and rule the bureaucracy. Because the Bush crowd doesn't like enforcement, they won't hesitate to take advantage of the institutional tension between program managers and EPA's enforcement staff. When industry (or its administration backers) feels persecuted, it complains to the program managers, who in turn give us an earful. Under Clinton, we were usually able to push back when we had to; if we declared something to be an enforcement matter, we'd often win the day. A good example of how the balance has shifted is the way the Bush administration stopped enforcing agricultural pollution regulations. American agriculture is big business, comparable in scale to the refineries and steel plants that typically occupy the EPA's enforcement program. Most of the pork, beef, and poultry that Americans consume comes from factory farms where huge numbers of animals are massed together, creating waste that is widely recognized as one of the greatest threats to water quality. A large corporate hog farm churns out as much nitrogen-rich waste as a city the size of St. Louis—but without any wastewater treatment. In addition to fouling creeks and contaminating groundwater, studies show that gaseous ammonia, hydrogen sulfide, and other pollutants create serious respiratory problems for people living nearby. Few of these companies bother to obtain the required permits. So during the Clinton administration, the enforcement staff began cracking down, insisting, for example, that big hog farms monitor air emissions at sites where we had complaints. Yet when Bush officials took over, my office was asked to stop enforcing air pollution laws against waste lagoons and barns at factory farms, in favor of "voluntary studies," promoted by program bureaucrats.

Pack the courts. Like most conservatives, Bush understands the importance of packing the judiciary with right-wing jurists, as his predecessors did from 1981 to 1993. A look at just one case illustrates how a conservative court can shrink the laws meant to protect the environment. Not long ago, the EPA tried to stop developers from using a tricky technique that undermines the Clean Water Act, which prohibits the filling of wetlands. Unscrupulous developers had learned they could simply drain thousands of acres of this ecologically valuable habitat by using perforated, triangular-bladed plows that punch drainage ditches into swamps. Once the swamps have been drained, they're no longer a "water of the U.S." protected by federal law. When the D.C. Circuit Court of Appeals upheld this practice, it spurred a gold rush of development in sensitive coastal areas like the Great Dismal Swamp [in Virginia and North Carolina]. Developers drained about 20,000 acres of wetlands in the short space of a few months before the EPA began arguing that the sediment-choked water rushing off these drainage sites and into nearby streams violated other provisions of the statute.

After the 1994 GOP [Republican] takeover of Congress, it suddenly became acceptable for lawmakers to interfere . . . on behalf of constituent polluters.

Turn lawmakers into lobbyists. Bush will be able to count on the help of congressional right-wingers who love law and order, except when it upsets their campaign contributors. In August 1994, under a Democratic Congress, I was hauled before the majority staff of the Energy and Commerce Committee and warned not to give in to industries lobbying for "privilege" laws that shield evidence from environmental prosecutors. We had no intention of doing so, since in its most extreme form these privilege laws would make it easier for a company to hide evidence of criminal violations like deliberately dumping toxic waste down a drain, just by claiming the problem had been fixed. Six months later, following the Republican takeover, the EPA was attacked by the new majority for successfully rejecting privilege laws. Overnight, the EPA became "jackbooted thugs," in [Texas representative] Tom DeLay's famous construction. The oversight roles were reversed. Suddenly, Congress was attacking us for too much enforcement, not too little.

Individual congressmen have always gone to bat for local industries; but after the 1994 GOP [Republican] takeover of

Congress, it suddenly became acceptable for lawmakers to interfere aggressively in the enforcement process on behalf of constituent polluters, to a degree unheard of a decade ago. This trend has encouraged lawmakers to step in and act as defense lawyers on behalf of home state industries or political contributors. In my favorite example, [in 2001] we received identical form letters from more than 20 different members of Congress within a two-week period, parroting the sound bites that industry lobbyists used to persuade the Bush administration to stall enforcement actions against utility companies. These members, too lazy to even alter the wording of the letter they were handed by some lobbyist, had no clue what the government's position was. They had never requested a briefing.

Congressional oversight isn't always bad. Recently, at the behest of an oil company trying to slow down enforcement action, a senator forced us to catalogue all of the "information requests" we had issued to companies suspected of violating certain Clean Air Act requirements, which led us to create a better inventory of these data and forced us to think about focusing our requests. We had to face the fact that some of our information requests were sloppier than they should have been, and that we were taking too long to review the information asked for. But as with so many other trends, congressional interference has gotten markedly worse under Bush. Congressmen have become de facto lobbyists for home state polluters.

Dump it on the states. According to Bush doctrine, what little environmental enforcement is necessary should be left to states. In theory, states issue most permits for air and water pollution and waste management because they have been shown capable of running such programs as required by federal law. In practice, EPA's records are so incomplete that it has little clue how well most states perform. Some, like New York, driven by Attorney General Eliot Spitzer, have outstanding enforcement programs. But periodic reviews by the General Accounting Office [now called the Government Accountability Office] and the Inspector General repeatedly expose systematic failures to issue permits, track compliance, find violations, and prosecute them effectively. In addition to lacking resources, many states, especially in the South and West, are hostile to the very idea that most environmental laws should be enforced. State officials see red when EPA steps in to take enforcement action (allowed by federal law) against one of "their" businesses. Some of this is jurisdictional—aren't the local cops on TV always complaining about the FBI? But the constant and petty turf battles with state political managers were one of my most dispiriting experiences. On several occasions, state agencies, informed of an EPA investigation, rushed to cut a sweetheart deal with the target company to obviate the federal case. Once, over drinks, a state enforcement manager confessed to me that his governor had instructed him to bash the federal EPA, no matter what it did. This has always been a problem, but Clinton officials were less likely to pretend that states could do everything.

> *While the president talks ceaselessly about innovation, partnerships, and voluntary programs in public, privately his administration . . . challenges . . . any worthwhile environmental rule.*

This devolution to state enforcement also serves the administration's corporate sponsors, since states are consistently more cooperative and lenient than the federal EPA. It's no small irony that Administrator Whitman, when she was governor of New Jersey, eliminated the state environmental prosecutor and made deep cuts in New Jersey's enforcement budget.

The innovation fetish. Under Clinton, the EPA reasoned that the best way to get polluters to comply with the law was to sue whole industries, not just individual companies. Under Bush, that reasoning has cleverly been reversed. If entire industries are not complying with environmental laws, goes the Bush philosophy, then there must be something wrong with the laws.

This philosophy exploits another EPA tic: The tendency to spend more time writing new regulations and guidance than enforcing existing laws, a pattern already causing problems for the enforcement staff under Clinton. The EPA is divided between program staff, who devise the regulations, and enforcement staff, who implement them. Program officers don't simply write the rules and move on; they are under constant pressure to revise the regulations. In theory, this is a fine thing. Regulations, like anything else in life, can be improved. The problem, however, is that the process by which the "new and improved" regulations are approved is dysfunctional. It [is] dragging on forever because of the agency's obsession with "consensus." Any new proposal must wind its way through a labyrinth of political appointees and "stakeholders" (the euphemism for lobbyists). At the end of this maze sits the famously political Office of Management and Budget and the White House, both eager to second-guess any decision. When I first came to enforcement in the spring of 1997, EPA was deep in the process of rewriting the rules that prohibit sewer overflow and discharges from farm factories. Years later, it is still struggling just to propose these same rules for comment.

To survive this obstacle course, EPA program managers have become acutely sensitive to anything that will upset the apple cart. Such a system discourages tough environmental enforcement. My staff and I routinely fielded calls from program managers or their senior staff, irate that some enforcement action threatened to derail a pending rule that would make existing prohibitions on pollution more "flexible."

And all this is worsening under Bush. While the president talks ceaselessly about innovation, partnerships, and voluntary programs in public, privately his administration questions the costs and challenges the benefits of any worthwhile environmental rule. The White House will not hesitate to step in and tell EPA how to write a rule, especially when it benefits the energy industry. As happened under [President] Ronald Reagan 20 years ago, the process of environmental enforcement has once again been intensely politicized. Today, major proposals setting standards for polluters are often little more than a collage of industry positions—and with the dearth of independent data or information, there's no way to show that the agency is working in the public interest.

Congress Has Failed to Push for Environmental Progress

Roy Bigham

Roy Bigham is managing editor of Pollution Engineering, *a magazine for environmental professionals that provides coverage of technical news about air, water, solid, and hazardous waste pollution.*

As Congress bickers about Social Security, health care, energy and other issues, it has done little about upgrading environmental issues. Sure, they tossed a few tidbits into the energy bill that was passed [in 2005], but they also watered down much of it before it even exited committee.

Consider that the Clean Air Act (CAA) was last amended by Congress in 1990. The funding mechanism for Superfund [a toxic-waste cleanup program] was allowed to die in 1995. Congress and others argued long and hard about the Clear Skies Act legislation [proposed by President George W. Bush] in 2003, while lawsuits were filed to block EPA [Environmental Protection Agency] efforts to implement changes to the New Source Review (NSR) [a preconstruction permit program run by the EPA to ensure that industrial expansion does not create more pollution]. Congress did not act to come up with an alternative, while many claimed the current NSR rules should be sufficient if properly enforced.

A federal appeals court recently sided with 14 states and blocked EPA from going forward with new regulations that many claimed were more likely to increase pollution. The court ruled that EPA's changes violated the language of the CAA, and that any such change can be authorized only by Congress.

State Environmental Efforts

The result of what many states see as a failure by the federal agencies and Congress to act has been an effort by states to try to move forward on their own. California passed new emission rules on mobile sources [such as cars and trucks]. The federal government claimed that states could not do that, but the courts backed California and allowed other states to reference the California rules.

States have been requesting that additional steps be taken to further control air contaminants that not only contribute to smog and soot, but to potential global warming.

The EPA Administrator is required by the CAA to revise federal air quality standards for smog and soot at least every five years. In 1997, [then EPA administrator], Carol Browner issued tighter standards for air pollutants. These standards were quickly challenged by industry and a federal appeals court found that the rules were unconstitutional. The conflict continued until [U.S. Supreme Court] Justice Antonin Scalia ruled in 2001 that Browner did have the authority under the CAA to take the actions she did and had properly exercised that right. The regulations took effect at that time.

Since then, states have been requesting that additional steps be taken to further control air contaminants that not only contribute to smog and soot, but to potential global warming and health problems as well. The EPA responded that they did not have authority to place controls on gases such as CO_2 [carbon dioxide] under the CAA. They did respond to requests to lower mercury limits but some states believed the timeline to meet those standards was much too long and lenient. States such as Illinois are considering writing their own mercury control rules. This could lead to a jumble of standards for industry to meet.

It is now time for [current EPA administrator] Stephen L. Johnson to review and perhaps revise federal air quality standards for smog and soot. Scientists and environmental groups are taking umbrage at his proposals. They claim that the new particulate and soot standards are only a modest revision of the Browner rules and completely ignore the last few years of research, including some 2,000 studies that expand the list of adverse health effects associated with the fine particles, particularly for young children.

With all the confusion, it would be a good opportunity for Congress to step up and clarify some of the legal language in the CAA. It could also be a boost to our economy. As was stated in a *New York Times* editorial in January 2006, "while the standards do not deliver cleaner air on their own, they set in motion the regulatory machinery and capital investments aimed at achieving cleaner air."

The U.S. Environmental Protection Agency Is Allowing Factory Farms to Pollute Waterways

Amanda Griscom Little

Amanda Griscom Little writes a column on environmental politics and policy for Grist, *an environmental magazine. Her articles on energy and the environment have also appeared in publications ranging from* Rolling Stone *to the* New York Times Magazine.

The [George W.] Bush administration wants to let factory farms determine whether the animal excreta that oozes from their facilities into waterways should be regulated, environmentalists say—and they argue that the plan, well, stinks.

Factory Farms and Pollution

Agriculture has long been a top source of water pollution in the U.S., but in the last two decades the scale of the problem has grown dramatically with the proliferation of large-scale pork, poultry, beef, and dairy facilities, known as concentrated animal feeding operations (CAFOs). From 2002 to 2005, the CAFO industry in the U.S. expanded by about 22 percent—with substantially more animals per facility, and ever-larger piles of their droppings.

Today these facilities are responsible for some 500 million tons of animal manure a year—three times more waste than humans in this country produce, activists say. According to a 1998 report from the Department of Agriculture and U.S. EPA

[Environmental Protection Agency], CAFO muck has fouled roughly 35,000 miles of rivers in 22 states and groundwater in 17 states. More recent data show that 29 states have reported water contamination from these feedlots.

Bush Administration Proposals

[In June 2006], the EPA proposed a rule that purports to address this problem. It would revise a set of rules issued in 2003 that revamped the permitting process required of CAFOs under the Clean Water Act, with the aim of better tracking discharge levels at each facility and holding factory farms accountable for their water pollution. The 2003 rules were deemed inadequate by the 2nd U.S. Circuit Court of Appeals [in 2005]. This decision was the upshot of a lawsuit filed by the Natural Resources Defense Council, the Sierra Club, and the Waterkeeper Alliance alleging that U.S. waterways aren't sufficiently protected from farm-animal feces, which can carry viruses, parasites, and bacteria such as *E. coli*. Says EPA spokesperson Dale Kemery, "The new rule complies with the 2nd Circuit decision, and will result in better Clean Water Act compliance among CAFOs."

But enviros disagree. "The court required the EPA to bring clarity to some aspects of the 2003 rules; instead they've created more confusion and new loopholes," says Michele Merkel, a former staff attorney in the EPA's enforcement division who now works for the nonprofit Environmental Integrity Project. The most concerning loophole, she says, would allow CAFOs themselves to define what constitutes a polluting discharge, and therefore decide whether a permit is needed at all.

Today the vast majority of factory farms still don't have permits for . . . pollution.

Such flexibility flies in the face of the Clean Water Act, says Merkel, because the law prohibits all large-scale feedlots from discharging any traceable animal waste into nearby waterways, and requires them to obtain permits that offer exemptions under certain circumstances, such as when there's runoff after a storm.

"The loophole basically renders the Clean Water Act meaningless when it comes to regulating the fecal discharge from CAFOs," says Merkel. "It says to these massive facilities, 'Hey, figure out if you need a permit to pollute, and then come and get one.' It's appalling."

The agriculture industry, meanwhile, is applauding the proposed rule. Don Parish, senior director of regulatory relations for the American Farm Bureau Federation, says it would lighten the regulatory burden on CAFOs. Obtaining permits, he says, is "an onerous process. When you have a permit, every 'i' that you don't dot and every 't' you don't cross is a problem, and creates substantial liability concerns." . . .

A Loosely Regulated Industry

There are plenty of means by which CAFO animal waste can make its way into waterways, according to Melanie Shepherdson, a staff attorney with the Natural Resources Defense Council's water and oceans program. The massive reservoirs in which the waste is stored, known as "lagoons," are vulnerable to routine leaks or occasionally significant breaks in their walls. Also, since the lagoons are commonly uncovered, nitrogen from the urine and excrement gasifies into the air, then redeposits onto the ground or nearby water bodies and can run off into further rivers and groundwater supplies. And the waste is commonly liquefied and sprayed onto a CAFO's surrounding fields, where it can likewise run off or leach into water sources.

"In 2003, EPA's position was that if you're a large-scale facility, it's nearly impossible not to have some amount of discharge," says Merkel "Therefore all large facilities should have permits." And yet today the vast majority of factory farms still don't have permits for this runaway pollution: Of the roughly 18,800 CAFOs currently in the United States, the EPA says only about 8,500 have permits.

Parish says this is just fine, arguing that the permitting process should not be mandatory for all CAFOs: "If you choose not to drive a car, does the government require you to have a driver's license? No. Likewise, if CAFOs do not discharge or intend to discharge, they shouldn't have to have a federal permit." The EPA adds that factory farms that send pollution into waterways without a permit risk punishment: "Under the Clean Water Act, CAFOs that do not seek permit coverage risk liability for any unpermitted discharges that may occur at the facility," says Kemery.

But there are troublingly few penalties being doled out, or even inspections taking place, says Merkel. Between 1997 and 2004, the U.S. Department of Justice waged a grand total of eight lawsuits against CAFOs for violating water-pollution standards under the Clean Water Act. "Without permits, government officials don't even know you're out there in many cases," says Merkel. Take the example of Illinois, she says, a major farm state where nearly 85 percent of the total public lake acreage is contaminated. "There are at least 500 large CAFOs in the state; only about 40 have permits, and only about a fifth of them have even been inspected," says Merkel. The state EPA has an inventory of only 30 percent of the CAFOs now operating in Illinois. "They don't even know where the vast majority are," says Merkel.

Says Shepherdson, "You'd be hard-pressed to find any other industry that is as loosely regulated as this one." She says it's no coincidence, noting that the ag industry is well-known for flexing its political muscle: "All of the big players have their trade groups out there on their behalf, lobbying both the EPA and friendly members of Congress to rewrite the [discharge] rules and exempt them from Clean Water Act requirements.

The EPA is clearly kowtowing to industry and abdicating its role as protector of public health."

The U.S. Environmental Protection Agency Claims It Has No Authority to Regulate Greenhouse Gases

Environment News Service

The Environment News Service is an independently owned and operated daily international wire service established in 1990 that offers news about the environment.

On [November 30, 2006,] the U.S. Supreme Court . . . [heard] oral arguments in a case that tests the authority of the U.S. Environmental Protection Agency, EPA, to regulate greenhouse gases from motor vehicles. Emitted by the combustion of oil and gas, greenhouse gases such as carbon dioxide are linked to global warming.

Massachusetts v. EPA

The case, *Massachusetts v. EPA* is brought against the EPA by 12 states, three cities and 13 environmental groups. They argue that the federal agency has an obligation to regulate greenhouse gases. The case turns on the EPA's 2003 decision that the agency has no legal authority under the federal Clean Air Act to regulate greenhouse gas emissions. This EPA ruling contradicts earlier statements and testimony from the agency, according to Massachusetts Attorney General Tom Reilly, Connecticut Attorney General Richard Blumenthal, and Maine Attorney General Steven Rowe. "EPA has long acknowledged the huge threats posed by global warming while refusing to do anything substantive about the problem," said Reilly. "EPA is claiming it actually has no authority to deal with the problem."

The [George W.] Bush administration argues that carbon dioxide is not a pollutant under the Clean Air Act, and that even if it were, the EPA has discretion over whether or not to regulate it. If the Court upholds the administration's position, it could jeopardize regulations enacted in California and 10 other states to require cuts in carbon dioxide emissions from motor vehicles.

Background of the Lawsuit

The case had its genesis in 1998, when the EPA's General Counsel found that the agency did have the authority to regulate the greenhouse gas carbon dioxide, CO_2, as an air pollutant. As a result, in 1999, the International Center for Technology Assessment, Sierra Club, Greenpeace and other environmental groups petitioned the EPA to set emissions limits for CO_2. The petition requested that EPA regulate carbon dioxide and other greenhouse gases emitted from new motor vehicles, concluding that it had a duty to do so under Section 202 of the Clean Air Act.

The EPA failed to respond after three years, resulting in a 2002 lawsuit brought by the environmental groups. In June 2003, Massachusetts, Connecticut and Maine filed a lawsuit which argued that by failing to regulate carbon dioxide, the dominant cause of global warming, EPA was violating its mandatory duty under Section 108 of the Clean Air Act.

In August 2003, the EPA withdrew and reversed its earlier position that carbon dioxide is an air pollutant subject to regulation under the Clean Air Act. In contrast to its prior position, EPA concluded that it lacks legal authority to regulate greenhouse gases. On the same day, EPA denied the petition for a rulemaking that environmental groups filed in 1999. EPA based its denial of the petition primarily upon its newly issued position that it lacks legal authority to regulate greenhouse gases.

After the EPA denied the petition to regulate carbon dioxide, the case moved to the U.S Court of Appeals for the D.C. Circuit. In October 2003, a coalition of 12 states, led by Massachusetts, along with the cities New York, Washington, DC, and Baltimore and 13 environmental groups, filed appeals in the U.S. Court of Appeals for the District of Columbia challenging both of EPA's August 2003 rulings. "The City of New York is proud to have joined in this appeal as part of my commitment to heed science—not political science—and try to counteract global warming," said New York Mayor Michael Bloomberg. "Climate change, rising sea levels, and increased storm surges attributable to growing greenhouse gas emissions put New Yorkers and New York's infrastructure at risk and pose serious challenges for our City's future," Bloomberg said. "Global warming threatens New York City and every city, and it is our duty to use this case and every other opportunity we have to prevent the situation from getting even worse."

A number of industry groups and states intervened in these appeals to support EPA's position. All of these appeals were consolidated into one case, *Commonwealth of Massachusetts, et al. v. EPA.* On July 15, 2005, a three-judge panel of the D.C. Circuit issued three separate opinions in the case. Two of the judges agreed to let EPA's administrative decision stand, but on very different grounds. The third judge, Judge David Tatel, issued a lengthy dissent agreeing with the Massachusetts position on all grounds. On August 29, 2005, Attorney General Reilly, together with five other states and the District of Columbia, asked the D.C. Circuit panel and the full court to rehear the case. On December 2, 2005, the court denied rehearing by the panel by a 2–1 vote, and denied full court review by a 4–3 vote. On March 2, 2006, Attorney General Reilly filed a petition asking the Supreme Court to accept the case. On June 26, 2006, the Supreme Court agreed to hear the case.

"For six years, the Bush administration and its friends in Congress have fought tooth and nail to avoid doing anything to fight global warming," said Carl Pope, Sierra Club's executive director. "We cannot wait for EPA to start following the law and take the important steps it must to fight global warming. We are confident that the Court will tell EPA to stop making excuses and rewriting the law as the administration sees fit and start working to protect the American people."

Editor's Note: On April 2, 2007, in a 5-4 decision, the Supreme Court ruled against the government in *Massachusetts v. EPA*, finding that the EPA does have the authority to regulate greenhouse gases in automobile emissions. On May 14, 2007 President George W. Bush responded to the decision by issuing an Executive Order ordering federal agencies to begin regulating greenhouse gas emissions from cars and trucks before he leaves office in January 2009.

The United States Can Grow the Economy and Protect the Environment at the Same Time

George W. Bush

George W. Bush is the forty-third president of the United States who began his second term on January 20, 2005.

Our nation faces some great challenges. The biggest challenge we face is the security of our people. We've got to make sure that America is secure from the enemies which hate us. And we've got to make America secure by having an economy that grows so people can find work. . . .

When I first got in in Washington, I put out a plan, a national energy strategy. . . . Part of that plan modernizes—calls for the modernization of the electricity grid. We need more investment; we need research and development to make sure we're—as we invest new technologies, they're the latest and best for the people of this country. We also want to make sure voluntary reliability standards for utilities are now mandatory reliability standards. When somebody says they're going to be reliable, we don't want it to be maybe reliable or perhaps reliable, we want mandatory reliability standards, so people can count on the deliver—to have their electricity delivered. . . . We've [also] got to make sure that the energy we use, we have the best technologies to make sure we burn it as clean as we can. That's why I have a strong initiative for clean coal technology. We want to make sure we encourage conservation. But the truth of the matter is, we need to become less dependent on foreign sources of energy. For the sake of economic security.

George W. Bush, President's remarks at Detroit Edison Monroe Power Plant in Monroe, Michigan, www.whitehouse.gov, September 15, 2003. www.whitehouse.gov/news/releases/2003/09/20030915-6.html. Reproduced by permission.

Protecting Jobs and the Environment

We lead the world in new technologies when it comes to energy, and we not only can find new ways of producing energy and make sure we do so in an efficient way, we can make sure we do so in a clean way. You know right here what I'm talking about at this plant. We lead the world in technologies to make the production of energy cleaner. And so therefore, I'm confident in predicting to the American people [that] not only can we promote job security and increase jobs, but we can do so in way that protects our environment. And I believe we have a duty to do so. I believe a responsible nation is one that protects the environment.

There's reason for [our economic and environmental] progress, and it's because our nation made a commitment; starting in the Clean Air Act of 1970, we set high goals.

Yet the government sometimes doesn't help. And that's what I'm here to discuss: those moments when the government doesn't help, when the government stands in the way. For example, power plants are discouraged from doing routine maintenance because of government regulations. And by routine maintenance, I mean replacing worn-out boiler tubes or boiler fans. And all that does is it makes the plant less reliable, less efficient and not as environmentally friendly as it should be. So I changed those regulations, my administration did. . . .

I said as plainly as I could that I believe we can grow our economy and protect the quality of our air at the same time. And we made progress doing just that. Let me give you a statistic or two. Our economy has grown 164 percent in three decades. That's pretty good growth. And yet, according to a report that the EPA is [has released], air pollution from six major pollutants is down by 48 percent during that period of time. So you nearly double your economy and yet pollution is down by nearly 50 percent.

That should say to people that we can grow our economy, that we can work to create the conditions for job growth, and that we can be good stewards of the air we breathe. And this plant [the Detroit Edison Monroe Power Plant in Monroe, Michigan,] is a good example of that achievement. Since 1974, the power generated from here has increased by 22 percent. You've created more power, so more people can live a decent life. And yet, the particulant [*sic*] matter emissions have fallen by 80–81 percent. You're good stewards of the quality of the air, as well. You work hard in this plant to put energy on the grid, and at the same time, you're protecting the environment.

There's reason for this progress, and it's because our nation made a commitment; starting in the Clean Air Act of 1970, we set high goals. We said this is a national priority. Let's work together to achieve these priorities. And we are working together. This administration, my administration, strongly supports the Clean Air Act, and I believe that by combining the ethic of good stewardship—in other words, convince people that it's an important goal—and the spirit of innovation, we will improve the quality of our air even further. And at the same time, make sure people can find a job.

Steps to Cleaner Air

There is more to do, and so I want to talk about three ideas that—three common-sense steps that I put out to help us meet the new air quality standards and further improve quality of life. I hope you find that they make sense. They certainly do to me. They're common-sense ways to deal with our environment.

First, we're going after the pollution that comes from diesel vehicles. We worked with the energy companies and the agricultural concerns and the manufacturers; we worked with environment groups; we worked with union groups—to come up with a common-sense policy. And we did, we developed one. It's now being implemented. Oil companies will lower the sulfur in diesel fuel. We'll enforce new emission limits on diesel truck engines. And we're going to put forward new rules that will control pollution from off-road vehicles like heavy construction equipment. . . .

Instead of the government telling utilities where and how to cut pollution, we will work with them to create a cap . . . [but let them] figure out how.

Secondly, I proposed what's called Clear Skies legislation. . . . Clear Skies legislation will help cut power plant emissions, without affecting job growth and/or jobs at this plant. We're interested in reducing the nitrogen oxide, sulfur dioxide [and] mercury, coming out of the power plants around America. We've put forth a plan, we brought people in a room, we discussed it with them. The stakeholders agreed; union workers—union leaders have agreed; utilities have agreed; manufacturing companies have agreed to a plan that will reduce those three key pollutants by 70 percent over a reasonable period of time.

We've got an interesting approach—it's been tried in the past, it's a cap and trade system. We put mandatory caps on emissions. It's a little different look than maybe you're used to. Instead of the government telling utilities where and how to cut pollution, we will work with them to create a cap, how much to cut, and when we expect it cut by, but you figure out how. You're a lot better in figuring out the how than people in Washington, D.C. Each year each facility will need a permit for each ton of pollution it emits. Companies that are able to reduce their pollution below the amount can sell the surplus to others that need more time to meet the national goal and the national standard. In other words, there's an incentive system built into it. The system makes it worthwhile for companies to invest earlier in controls, and therefore, pollute less. It ensures that high standards are met in a common-sense way that is cost-effective and saves jobs. And under the legislation, communities that have had trouble meeting air quality standards will finally have a clear and a more effective method to get them help.... Clear Skies is good, sound legislation and needs to be passed.

We've issued new rules that will allow utility companies ... to make routine repairs and upgrades without enormous costs and endless disputes.

New Regulations

Finally, I want to speak to one other matter. It's called New Source Review. We need to fix those—and have—we're in the process of fixing what they call New Source Review regulations. After I explain it, I think it will make sense as to why we're doing it. The old regulations ... undermined our goals for protecting the environment and growing the economy. The old regulations on the books made it difficult to either ... protect the environment or grow the economy. Therefore, I wanted to get rid of them. I'm interested in job creation and clean air, and I believe we can do both.

One of the things we've got to do is encourage companies to invest in new technologies, convince utilities to modernize their equipment, so that they can produce more energy and pollute less. In other words, as technologies come on, we want to encourage companies to make investment in those technologies. Yet old regulations, the ones we're change—changing, actually discourage companies from even making routine repairs and replacing old equipment. That's the reality. Regulations intended to enhance air quality made it really difficult for companies to do that which is necessary, to not only produce more energy, but to do it in a cleaner way.

Power plants and companies wanted to make one change they could afford. The regulators could come in and order them to change everything, making every change a massive, multi-year battle. That's the reality here at Monroe plant. The people who are trying to modernize this plant and do their job on behalf of the people of Michigan found out that the regulations were so complex that they could be interpreted any different way. And that's what happened. And when you have complex regulations that are open for interpretation, guess what happens? The lawyers come in. And then you have litigation, and then things grind to a standstill. So a lot of planners and people who were charged with providing electricity and to protect the air decided not to do anything. They didn't want to have to fight through the bureaucracy or fight through the endless lawsuits. And when that happens, fewer power plants are upgraded; they become old and tired—which means people start losing their jobs; which means our economy is not robust so people can find work if they're looking for work; which means in some cases, energy costs are higher than they should be. . . .

And so . . . we decided to do something about it. We began to review the old rules and regulations. And we wanted to do so in a careful way. The EPA held five public meetings. More than 100 groups were represented, citizens and industry and local officials. There were thousands of comments. In other words, we said, if you've got a problem with the change, please bring them forward; or you support the change, bring them forward. We wanted to hear from people. And the EPA did a good job of collecting data. In December [2002], we issued the first set of rules to clarify and simplify regulations for manufacturers to do projects in an energy-efficient way and to promote policy that would discourage pollution. And now we've issued new rules that will allow utility companies, like this one right here, to make routine repairs and upgrades without enormous costs and endless disputes. We simplified the rules. We made them easy to understand. We trust the people in this plant to make the right decisions.

There is a lot of debate about New Source Review—the change of New Source Review. It makes sense to change these regulations. It makes sense for the workplace environment; it makes sense for the protection of our air. Not only do I believe that, but union leaders believe that, manufacturers believe that, the utilities believe that, a bipartisan coalition in Congress believes it. We have done the right thing. Monroe plant is a living example of why we acted. The people at this plant wanted to put the most modern equipment, use the most modern technology to make [sure] the people of Michigan got energy at a reasonable and affordable price, and at the same time protect the environment. Government policy prevented them from doing so. We have changed the government policy for [the] good of the people of this country.

I mentioned the challenges we face, but I'm an optimist, because I understand America. It's been my privilege to see the character of the American people. We are resolute. We're plenty tough when we have to be tough. We're also compassionate. Ours is a resourceful nation; we set goals and we work together to achieve those goals. Ours is a nation that when we hear that somebody is looking for work and can't find work, cares about that person.

I want to make sure this environment, economic environment of ours is as healthy as it can be. The American people have got to understand a healthy economic environment means we'd better have energy; we'd better be producing that energy, there's electricity, so people can expand their manufacturing facilities. If you've got an issue with the manufacturing base, you'd better make sure you've got a reliable supply of energy for the manufacturers, like they've got here in Michigan.

We can overcome problems. We're smart and resourceful people. We're also a compassionate people, people who are willing to love a neighbor just like we love ourselves. That's what I love most about America. I love the fact that there are people who hurt—I love the fact that when somebody is hurting in your neighborhood, you're likely to walk across the street and say, what can I do to help? It's a fabulous country we have. Oh, yes, we've got problems. There's no doubt in my mind, because of the character of the American people, we can overcome any problem that's in our way.

The United States Is Enforcing the Montreal Treaty to Protect the Ozone Layer

Environmental Protection Agency

The Environmental Protection Agency is a federal agency charged with protecting human health and preserving the natural environment of the United States.

Hydrochlorofluorocarbons, or HCFCs, are a class of chemical compounds that are mainly used as refrigerants in the air-conditioning and refrigeration industries. They are also important components for foam blowing, solvent cleaning, and fire protection. Because HCFCs play a role in depleting the ozone layer the United States is phasing out their consumption by first limiting and then ending their production and import in particular. HCFC-22 and HCFC-142b are the next two HCFCs that the United States will phase out.

HCFC-22 and HCFC-142b

HCFC-22 is also referred to as R-22 or by one of its trade names, Freon® 22. It is a popular refrigerant that is commonly used in a variety of refrigeration and air-conditioning equipment. . . .

HCFC-142b, or R-142b, is also used as a refrigerant. HCFC-142b is rarely used by itself; it is generally a component of a refrigerant blend. For example, it is part of a blend known as R-409A, which also includes HCFC-22. HCFC-142b is also used for foam blowing and as a propellant in aerosol cans.

Other commonly used HCFCs include HCFC-123, HCFC-124, HCFC-225Ca, and HCFC-225cb. . . .

Environmental Protection Agency, "Phaseout of HCFC-22 and HCFC-142b in the United States: Frequently Asked Questions," 2007. www.epa.gov/ozone/title6/phaseout/hcfcfaqs.html#why_epa. Reproduced by permission.

Why Does EPA Regulate HCFCs?

The stratospheric ozone layer shields the Earth from the sun's harmful ultraviolet (UV) radiation. Overexposure to UV radiation can cause skin cancer and cataracts or damage crops and materials. However, emissions of manmade chemicals that contain chlorine and bromine—including chlorofluorocarbons, halons, and hydrochlorofluorocarbons—destroy the ozone layer, and have created an "ozone hole" over the South Pole.

Reversing ozone depletion is crucial to human and environmental health worldwide. In 1988, the United States ratified the Montreal Protocol on Substances that Deplete the Ozone Layer. By ratifying the Protocol and its amendments, the United States committed to a collaborative, international effort to regulate and phase out ozone-depleting substances. This effort is expected to result in the recovery of the ozone layer by the middle of this century to pre-1980 levels, as long as all countries meet their established targets.

Under the Montreal Protocol, the United States must first limit HCFC consumption (production and import) to a specific level and then reduce it in a step-wise fashion. In developing the phaseout schedule for each ozone-depleting substance, the United States considers each substance's relative contribution to ozone depletion, or its ozone depletion potential. The Parties to the Montreal Protocol created a schedule with graduated reductions of HCFC production and import and eventual phaseout (of production, not use) by January 1, 2030. . . .

U.S. Regulations to Phase Out HCFCs

The United States amended the Clean Air Act (CAA) in 1990 to include Title VI, Stratospheric Ozone Protection. The Montreal Protocol provided the basis for Title VI, which included additional requirements to phase out the production of substances that deplete the ozone layer. The U.S. has already phased out many substances and is now phasing out Class II Substances (the HCFCs) starting with those that have the greatest ozone depletion potential (ODP).

As of January 1, 2003, EPA banned production and import of HCFC-141b, the HCFC with the highest ODP. This action allowed the United States to reduce its consumption by 35 percent below the cap by the January 1, 2004, deadline and meet its obligations under the Montreal Protocol. In 2003 EPA issued baseline allowances for production and import of HCFC-22 and HCFC-142b. EPA allocated 100 percent of the U.S. consumption and production caps by allocating both consumption and production allowances to individual companies for HCFC-141b, HCFC-22, and HCFC-142b. . . .

Future Phaseout Action

As the next major step to phase out HCFCs, EPA will further limit the production and import of HCFC-22 and HCFC-142b. Starting January 1, 2010, the production and import of HCFC-22 or HCFC-142b for newly manufactured equipment will stop in the United States. The production/import limit will be set at a level that is suitable for servicing existing equipment. Only importers that have consumption allowances may import HCFC-22 and HCFC-142b, as described in the answers to frequently asked questions by chemical manufacturers, importers, and exporters. Between 2010 and 2020, HCFC-22 and HCFC-142b will be produced or imported for the exclusive purpose of servicing existing equipment. As of January 1, 2015, as part of the phaseout of all HCFCs, the sale and use of HCFC-22 and HCFC-142b will be banned except for transformation or servicing refrigeration and air-conditioning applications. EPA will not permit newly manufactured HCFC-22, HCFC-142b, or blends containing either substance, to be used for charging new equipment. Starting January 1, 2020, the production and import of HCFC-22 and HCFC-142b will be banned entirely in the United States. Once this happens, only recycled/reclaimed or stockpiled quantities of HCFC-22 and HCFC-142b will be available for servicing existing equipment. As of January 21, 2003, imports of HCFC-22, HCFC-141b, and HCFC-142b are restricted to holders of consumption allowances. Similarly, imports of all used HCFCs are restricted to those who have obtained EPA approval prior to the shipments' export from the country of origin.

Reports Exaggerating
Air Pollution Risks
Needlessly Create Pressure
for More Regulation

Joel Schwartz

Joel Schwartz is a senior fellow in the Environment Program at the Reason Public Policy Institute. He also is a former executive officer of the California Inspection and Maintenance Review Committee, a government body charged with evaluating California's smog check program.

The United States has made dramatic progress in reducing air pollution over the last few decades, and most American cities now enjoy relatively good air quality. But polls show that most Americans believe air pollution has grown worse or will become worse in the future, and that most people face serious risks from air pollution.

Exaggerated Claims of Air Pollution Risks

This disconnect between perception and reality is, in part, the result of environmental activists' exaggerations of air pollution levels and risks, which make air pollution appear to be increasing when in fact it has been declining. State and federal regulatory agencies sometimes also resort to such tactics, and the media generally report those claims uncritically. As a result, public fears over air pollution are out of all proportion to the actual risks posed by current air pollution levels, and there is widespread but unwarranted pessimism about the nation's prospects for further air pollution improvements.

If people overestimate their exposure to and risk from air pollution, they will demand stricter, more costly air pollution

Joel Schwartz, "Clearing the Air," *Regulation*, vol. 26, no. 2, summer 2003, pp. 22–24, 29. www.cato.org/pubs/regulation/v26n2-4.pdf.

regulation. We face many threats to our health and safety, but have limited resources with which to address them; by devoting excessive resources to one exaggerated risk, we are less able to counter other genuinely more serious risks. People can make informed decisions about air pollution control only if they have accurate information on the risks they face.

The Reality

The Environmental Protection Agency [EPA] monitors ozone and other air pollutants at hundreds of locations around the United States. EPA has two ozone standards: The first, known as the "one-hour standard," requires that daily ozone levels exceed 125 parts per billion (ppb) on no more than three days in any consecutive three-year period. Ozone levels are determined based on hourly averages (hence the name of the standard). EPA's "eight-hour standard," promulgated in 1997, is more stringent. It requires that the average of the fourth-highest daily, eight-hour average ozone level from each of the most recent three years not exceed 85 ppb. The standards are difficult to compare because of their different forms, but the one-hour standard is roughly equivalent to an eight-hour standard set at about 95 ppb.

[The] downward trend in pollution levels will continue.

In the early 1980s, half of the nation's monitoring stations registered ozone in excess of the federal one-hour health standard, and they averaged more than 12 such exceedances per year. But as of the end of 2002, only 13 percent of the stations failed the one-hour standard and they averaged just four exceedances per year. . . .

The nation's success with air quality extends beyond ozone to other pollutants. For example, between 1981 and 2000, carbon monoxide (CO) declined 61 percent, sulfur dioxide (SO_2) 50 percent, and nitrogen oxides (NO_x) 14 percent. Only two among hundreds of the nation's monitoring locations still exceed the CO and SO$_2$ standards. All areas of the country meet the NO$_x$ standard. For all three pollutants, pollution levels are well below the EPA standards in almost all cases.

Likewise, airborne particulate matter (PM) has also registered large declines. PM$_{2.5}$ (PM up to 2.5 microns in diameter) dropped 33 percent from 1980 to 2000, while the soot emissions rate from diesel trucks is down almost 85 percent since 1975.

Future Decline

This downward trend in pollution levels will continue. On-road pollution measurements show per-mile emissions from gasoline vehicles are dropping by about 10 percent per year as the fleet turns over to more recent models that start out and stay much cleaner than vehicles built years ago. Diesel truck emissions are also declining, albeit about half as fast. Although motorists are driving more miles each year and population growth means more motorists on the roads, the increases in driving are tiny compared to the large declines in vehicle emission rates and will do little to slow progress on auto pollution.

Despite past success in reducing air pollution and the positive outlook for the future, polls show most Americans think air pollution is getting worse.

Emissions from industrial sources will also continue to drop. Starting in 2004, EPA regulations require a 60 percent reduction in warm-season NO$_x$ emissions from coal-fired power plants and industrial boilers—the major industrial sources of ozone-forming pollution. The federal Clean Air Act requires a 20 percent reduction in PM-forming SO$_2$ from power plants between 2000 and 2010. Those reductions are in addition to substantial declines in industrial NO_x and SO_2 emissions over the last 30 years.

Misperceptions

Despite past success in reducing air pollution and the positive outlook for the future, polls show most Americans think air pollution is getting worse. . . .

According to the old saying, "It's not the things we didn't know that hurt us; it's the things we knew for sure that turned out to be wrong." When it comes to air pollution, why do most Americans "know" so much that is not so? Americans consider environmental groups the most credible source of information on the environment, yet those activist groups consistently provide misleading information on air pollution levels, trends, risks, and prospects. Americans also trust information from regulatory agencies, yet the agencies often paint a misleadingly pessimistic picture. At the same time, the media often provide extensive coverage of air pollution reports and press releases from environmentalists and government regulators, yet the press reports rarely include critical examination or context on the claims those organizations make. . . .

Exaggerating health risks from air pollution can be as bad as minimizing them.

Most Americans trust information from environmentalists and government agencies. A 1999 poll commissioned by the American Lung Association found that 90 percent of people trust environmental information provided by the association (59 percent of them a "great deal") while 79 percent trust EPA. A 2002 poll commissioned by the Sierra Club found that 57 percent of Americans trust environmental groups for information on environmental issues. As we have seen, that trust is misplaced.

Wasted Resources

Exaggerating health risks from air pollution can be as bad as minimizing them. Either extreme results in wasted resources and diversion of people's attention from more serious risks. Unwarranted alarmism also causes unnecessary public fear. The public's interest is in an accurate portrayal of risk. People ultimately bear regulatory costs through reductions in their disposable income because regulations increase the costs of producing useful goods and services. A large body of research shows that, on average, people use their disposable income to increase health and safety for themselves and their loved ones. A regulation will improve people's health only if the health benefits of the regulation exceed the harm caused by the regulation's income-reducing costs.

Regulators and environmentalists no doubt appear to be more credible sources of objective information when compared with, say, politicians or industry lobbyists. But, like other interest groups, the goals of regulators and activists often do not coincide with the interests of the vast majority of Americans. Environmental groups want to increase support for ever-more-stringent regulations and bring in the donations that support their activism. And while regulators want to show the success of their efforts to reduce air pollution, they also want to justify the need to preserve or expand their powers and budgets. Maintaining a climate of crisis and pessimism meets those institutional goals, but at the expense of encouraging the public to exaggerate its risk.

Air pollution levels, trends, and health effects are complex issues, yet journalists and editors face many constraints in trying to interpret environmental information for the public. Reporters often do not have specific subject expertise, and may not feel comfortable trying to sort out the nuances and complexities that lie behind proponents' portrayals of environmental data. Time and space limitations often prevent or discourage efforts to seek out experts who could critically evaluate particular claims.

Yet if the media are unable or unwilling to improve environmental reporting, the public is likely to remain misinformed. At the very least, reporters and editors must begin to treat claims by ostensible "do-gooders"—environmentalists, regulators, and even university researchers—with the same skepticism appropriate for other interested parties in regulatory debates.

Increased Energy Efficiency Is Reducing CO$_2$ Emissions and Slowing Global Warming

Patrick J. Michaels

Patrick J. Michaels is a senior fellow in environmental studies at the Cato Institute, a libertarian think tank, and author of the 2004 book, Meltdown: The Predictable Distortion of Global Warming by Scientists, Politicians, and the Media.

R eaders of recent news reports may think it's news that U.S. emissions of carbon dioxide, the main global-warming gas, are at an all-time high. The real news would be if they dropped steeply, which could only occur with a very warm winter (less space heating), a very cold summer (less air conditioning) or a huge recession, because it takes energy to make things.

Carbon dioxide has been called the breath of our civilization, and as we are technologically constituted, it most certainly is. We burn fossil fuels (which combust mainly to carbon dioxide and water) for manufacturing, to go places, and to produce electrical power. While we could certainly substitute in more nuclear fuels for power production, the same forces that are so exercised about global warming being caused by carbon dioxide, in general, won't permit the nuclear option. (That being the definition of environmental insincerity.) So it is not news at all that our emissions are at a record high along with GDP [gross domestic product].

Improvements in Energy Efficiency

What is more newsworthy is how the emissions per unit of GDP—the economic bang for the energy buck—continue their steady decline. We now produce a constant dollar's worth

Patrick J. Michaels, "Warming to Efficiency," *The American Spectator*, January 18, 2006. Copyright © *The American Spectator* 2006. Reproduced by permission.

of goods and services with only 78% of the energy we used in 1990. In 1990, we used about two-thirds of the energy we used in 1970 for the same dollar's worth. These are remarkable increases in efficiency in the last 35 years.

The *New York Times* recently reported that the 2004 change in overall emissions was nearly double the annual average, neglecting to report that single-year statistics are virtually meaningless. If one had taken the average of the last five years and compared that to figures generated back to the mid-'90s, percent changes in emissions of carbon dioxide turn out to be remarkably constant. For 1999–2004 the increase averaged 0.8% per year. From 1996 through 2001 the change averaged 1.0%. Given year-to-year fluctuations, these numbers are indistinguishable from each other.

The same applies on a global scale. Our computer models for global warming have assumed, for decades, that carbon dioxide would increase at 1% per year in the atmosphere. For those decades the real rate of increase has been quite constant, and less than half of 1%. In the ten years ending in 2004, the average rate of increase was 0.49%. Ten years before it was 0.41%, and ten years before that, 0.42%. This is why climate models have generally predicted too much warming, too fast— about twice as much, in fact.

Taken together, all of these facts mean that most of the assumptions about the growth of global warming gases in the atmosphere have to be thrown out. There's little, if any, exponential increase, and the vibrant economies continue to produce more and more things with fewer increments of carbon dioxide.

The Future: Lower Carbon Emissions

But, if carbon dioxide is the cost of economic growth, it would seem obvious that it will continue its upwards ascent for the foreseeable future. Will it? The answer lies in the well-established trends towards increasing efficiency in economies such as the United States'. . . . This did not happen here because of concerns about global warming—because no one really gave much of a care about it until New Orleans got smacked by a Category 3 (yes, it's been downgraded) hurricane. Instead, the increases in efficiency resulted because businesses compete with each other to produce things that cost less to run and build. And, if they are built, people will come. And so do investors.

As an example of this process, get on your Yahoo financial tracker and plot the stock performance of Honda, Toyota, GM and Ford for the last two years. You'll find the share price of the producers of the Accord and the Camry up an average of 40% while the American companies have dropped 50% in value.

This creates a snowball effect in a warming world. People in vibrant economies have capital to invest in increasingly efficient companies, which rewards them with more capital, which is re-invested etc. The prospering companies are efficient in many ways. They use less energy to produce cars in their newer plants. Their cars use less energy on the road. Their labor forces tend to be relatively young and they haven't been promised the moon in benefits and retirement with 40% of their time on earth left to run.

As these companies accumulate capital, they have been re-investing it in development of even more efficient vehicles, some of which may emit no carbon dioxide at all, which means that some day the pressures for efficiency may indeed drive carbon dioxide emissions down. But, without investment in those technologies—made by private individuals in publicly traded corporations—be assured that development of the clean machines of the future will be delayed until the planet gets warmer than some might want it.

CHAPTER 4

What Are the Emerging Solutions to Environmental Pollution?

Chapter Preface

The Kyoto Protocol is part of the United Nations Framework Convention on Climate Change, an international treaty on global warning. The Kyoto amendments were negotiated in Kyoto, Japan, in December 1997 and went into effect in 2005. The protocol sets mandatory targets for the reduction of greenhouse gases—substances that scientists say are contributing to rising global temperatures—for developed countries that have signed and ratified the treaty.

The purpose of the Kyoto Protocol is for industrialized countries to reduce their total emissions of six greenhouse gases—carbon dioxide, methane, nitrous oxide, sulfur hexafluoride, haloalkanes, and perfluorocarbons—by 5.2 percent over the five-year period of 2008 to 2012, as compared with 1990 emission levels. Each participant, however, is assigned its own target goal; the European Union, for example, is expected to achieve an 8 percent reduction while Japan has a 6 percent goal and Russia is simply required to maintain its 1990 emissions level.

The protocol offers several incentives to encourage countries to comply. For example, it authorizes a "cap and trade" system, whereby countries and companies that expect to exceed their prescribed emissions limits may purchase emissions credits from other countries or companies that have more than met their expected emissions reductions. Another incentive is the Clean Development Mechanism, which allows developed countries to earn carbon credits for aiding projects that reduce greenhouse gases in developing countries; the other is Joint Implementation, a similar but smaller program that awards credits for environmentally friendly projects in problematic industrialized areas, such as central and eastern Europe.

As of the end of 2006, 169 countries had ratified the Kyoto agreement. Although the United States is the single-largest source of carbon emissions, responsible for about 25 percent of global greenhouse gases, U.S. presidents Bill Clinton and George W. Bush both refused to submit the agreement to the U.S. Senate for ratification. Both administrations objected to the treaty because it applied only to developed nations. The rapidly developing nation of the People's Republic of China, for example, is the world's second-largest emitter of greenhouse gases, but it and other developing countries, such as India, are not required to reduce carbon emissions under the terms of the present agreement. The U.S. position is that the treaty's failure to cover China and similar developing nations would place U.S. companies at a disadvantage and harm the U.S. economy. Australia, currently the second-largest carbon gas emitter, also refused to ratify the Kyoto Protocol.

Despite the U.S. refusal to ratify the Kyoto treaty, however, the Bush administration claims it is taking action to reduce U.S. greenhouse emissions. Officials with the U.S. Environmental Protection Agency (EPA), for example, claim that the United States has made progress in reducing some greenhouse gases, although U.S. carbon emissions have increased over recent years. The United States also has signed the Asia-Pacific Partnership on Clean Development and Climate, an agreement that provides for voluntary reductions of greenhouse gases. Critics of the Bush administration argue that these efforts are not enough, and claim that the administration is simply protecting the oil and gas industries.

In the absence of strong action at the federal level, several states and localities have pledged to set their own limits on greenhouse gas emissions. In 2006, for example, California passed legislation designed to reduce its greenhouse gas emissions by 25 percent by 2020. Since the state produces more emissions than many countries, California's effort, if successful, could significantly contribute to lower overall U.S. emission levels. At the bill's signing, California governor Arnold Schwarzenegger expressed the views of many when he stated, "We simply must do everything we can in our power to slow down global warming before it is too late.... The science is clear. The global warming debate is over."

Today, the Kyoto treaty faces an uncertain future. The lack of U.S. participation and the agreement's not covering rapidly developing countries are not the only obstacles. In addition, many signatory countries are having trouble meeting the treaty's emissions targets. Canada's emissions, for example, instead of shrinking to its target of 6 percent, have grown by 26 percent over 1990 levels. Japan, too, had a 6 percent goal, but is experiencing an 8.1 percent increase. Even the European Union expects to achieve 1 percent lower than its 8 percent target. Meanwhile, China's emissions have grown considerably, and it remains unregulated even though it is expected to overtake the United States as the world's largest source of greenhouse emissions by 2009, ten years earlier than once predicted. Moreover, even if the Kyoto treaty's goals were completely met by 2012, experts say this would reduce global temperatures only slightly, not enough to stop global warming or its harmful consequences.

In mid-November 2006, representatives from around the world met to discuss the future of the Kyoto targets after 2012, but no agreement was reached on future cuts. China and India both oppose placing emissions limits on developing countries, and the United States and Australia show no inclination to reverse their positions or join the treaty. Environmentalists say that both developed and developing nations must immediately act to limit global warming soon, or it will simply be too late to stop major climate change. The authors of the viewpoints in this chapter offer a variety of solutions for addressing today's environmental problems, including global warming.

More Must Be Done to Address Future Air Pollution Problems

National Academies

The National Academies is made up of the National Academy of Sciences, the National Academy of Engineering, the Institute of Medicine, and the National Research Council, and is a private, nonprofit group of distinguished scholars that provides science and technology advice to the public and policy makers under a congressional charter.

Despite the progress that has been made toward cleaner air in this country, more needs to be done to improve the nation's ability to confront future air pollution challenges, says a ... report from the National Academies' National Research Council [the principal operating arm of the National Academy of Sciences and the National Academy of Engineering].

Multipollutant, Result-Oriented Approach Necessary

The committee that wrote the report recommended that the U.S. Environmental Protection Agency [EPA] use an approach that targets groups of pollutants instead of individual ones. Revised or new regulations also should consider how air pollution travels from state to state and across international borders. Market-based approaches, such as emissions cap-and-trade programs—which set limits on the overall amount of emissions from industry but allow individual companies to buy and sell pollution "allowances"—should be used whenever

National Academies, "Clean Air Act Is Working, but Multipollutant, Multistate Approach and Stronger Focus on Results Are Needed to Meet Future Challenges" (press release), January 29, 2004. www8.nationalacademies.org/onpinews/newsitem.aspx ?RecordID=10728. Copyright © 2004 by the National Academy of Sciences, courtesy of the National Academies Press, Washington, DC. All rights reserved. Reproduced by permission.

practical and effective. And improved tracking of emissions is needed to accurately assess what populations are at the highest risk of health problems from pollution and to better measure the progress of pollution-control strategies.

The implementation of air quality regulations should be less bureaucratic—with more emphasis on results than process—and should be designed to protect ecosystems as well as people, the report says. Minority and low-income communities in dense urban settings may bear a disproportionate pollution burden, but these communities are not specifically targeted in the current Clean Air Act; they should be considered when regulations are revised, as should other environmental equity issues. Air quality standards also need to take into account climate change and the potential role of air pollutants in that change.

The committee grouped its proposals in five overarching and integrated recommendations that could be implemented in stages. EPA should form a task force to prepare a plan of action for implementing the report's recommendations and determining what legislative action is required to do so. In the meantime, EPA should maintain current programs to reduce pollution in the United States so that the progress toward cleaner air continues.

The country's air quality management system has made substantial progress since the [Clean Air Act] was passed in 1970.

Progress Under the Clean Air Act

At the request of Congress, the committee reviewed the effectiveness of the Clean Air Act and identified ways to improve its implementation. Overall, the committee found that the country's air quality management system has made substantial progress since the act was passed in 1970 and the creation of

EPA that same year. The act and its subsequent amendments target six major, or "criteria," pollutants—carbon monoxide, nitrogen dioxide, sulfur dioxide, ozone, particulate matter, and lead—as well as some other hazardous pollutants known as air toxics. Other goals of the act include improving visibility in wilderness areas and national parks, preventing acid rain, and curbing the use of chemicals that deplete the ozone layer.

Air quality standards established under the Clean Air Act and state implementation plans to meet those standards helped drive the development of new technologies that led to substantial decreases in pollution, the committee said. Networks that monitor air quality have documented decreases in concentrations of the criteria pollutants, and most parts of the country have achieved the standards for sulfur dioxide, nitrogen dioxide, and carbon monoxide. Eastern states have experienced a decline in the amount of sulfate deposited by acid rain. And several analyses show that the Clean Air Act has had, and will continue to have, a net economic benefit.

Areas for Improvement

The committee found several areas for improvement, however. It noted that standards tended to focus on single pollutants instead of using potentially more protective and cost-effective multipollutant strategies. Groups of pollutants that are emitted from similar sources, that can be controlled with related technologies, or that have a similar impact on public health, ecosystems, visibility, or global climate change should be regulated in a single approach, the committee said. For example, ozone, particulate matter, and a number of air toxics emitted by smokestacks and diesel engines could be targeted in the same regulation. Likewise, a single program could cover sulfur dioxide, mercury, and other pollutants that can be controlled at coal-fired power plants.

Future regulations also should be developed with greater consideration for how air pollution is transported from state to state and across international borders. Studies continue to indicate that air quality in a specific area can be influenced by pollutants that drift in from a different region, nation, or continent. The report says EPA should be given greater statutory responsibility and authority to deal with air quality problems in a regional, multistate context, especially since states obviously cannot control pollution that blows in from elsewhere.

Regulations for new cars and light trucks have greatly reduced vehicle emissions, but less progress has been made in reducing emissions from older heavy-duty diesel trucks, "nonroad" vehicles such as cranes and bulldozers, and malfunctioning automobiles. Also, while regulations governing new power plants and large factories have led to substantial reductions in emissions, many older plants remain a significant source of pollution, the report notes.

The committee said that the government's current risk assessments and standard-setting programs do not address all of the hazardous air pollutants that may pose a significant risk to people or the environment. There is increasing evidence that some criteria pollutants may cause adverse health effects even at very low levels of exposure; in fact, for some pollutants it may be impossible to set a minimum threshold below which there is no public health risk. And EPA's secondary standards, which aim to protect the environment, do not appear to be sufficient for protecting certain sensitive crops and ecosystems, the committee added.

Although concentrations of pollutants have decreased, many areas are not in compliance with newer, tougher standards for ozone and particulate matter, the committee noted. It added that the process states must follow to develop plans to meet standards has grown cumbersome and is too reliant on computer models whose ability to predict the effect of pollution-control strategies is uncertain. Rather than having to come up with multiple state implementation plans—each focused on a specific pollution standard—states should instead be asked to prepare an Air Quality Management Plan that encompasses all air quality activities in a single document, the report says.

Implementing the report's recommendations would require additional resources that would be significant but not overwhelming, the committee said. Even a doubling of the approximately $200 million EPA spends each year on air quality monitoring and research would be less than 1 percent of the annual expenditures nationwide for complying with the Clean Air Act, the committee noted. Much interdisciplinary research will be needed to bolster the scientific understanding necessary to implement the report's recommendations, which are intended to be adopted gradually so ongoing pollution prevention activities are not disrupted.

Manufacturers Must Design Products That Are Recyclable

Jackie Gubeno

Jackie Gubeno is an assistant editor at Recycling Today, *a monthly business magazine for the recycling industry.*

Smart investors know it's never a bad idea to plan for the future. The smartest seem to know that it's never too early to start.

Many manufacturers are starting to take a similar forward-looking attitude toward their products. Whether pushed by legislation or by competition to be environmentally friendly, many manufacturers are investing in the future by implementing Design for Recycling (DFR)—a policy the Institute of Scrap Recycling Industries Inc. (ISRI) has promoted that, as its name suggests, promotes designing products with their recyclability in mind from the very beginning.

By the Books

The DFR initiative was actually coined by the Institute of Scrap Iron and Steel (ISIS) in the early 1980s prior to the merger with the National Association of Recycling Industries (NARI) that created ISRI. The concept of Design for Recycling encompasses several aspects of manufacturing products with safe, easy recycling at their end of life in mind.

First and foremost, the policy encourages manufacturers to make sure consumer products can be safely and economically recycled. This includes eliminating or reducing hazardous or non-recyclable compounds used in products. ISRI's official policy position on Design for Recycling also states that

Jackie Gubeno, "Designs on the Future: Designing for Recycling Encourages Manufacturers to Plan for the End of Their Products' Lives," *Recycling Today*, vol. 44, no. 1, January 2006, pp. 86–89. Copyright © 2006 GIE Media, Inc. Reproduced by permission.

manufacturers who are required to redesign their products for better recycling should receive transitional assistance. "Manufacturers should not be asked to bear all the costs of Design for Recycling any more than recyclers should be required to continue to bear all the environmental risks of recycling in the absence of appropriate product design," states the ISRI policy page on the topic.

Recently, encouraging manufacturers to think about the recyclability of their products has taken a legislative bent, with the approval of two state bills addressing mercury switches in automobiles. An Arkansas law enacted in early 2005 is the first law on the books in the United States that requires manufacturers to address DFR issues, according to Mark Reiter, chief lobbyist for ISRI. In addition to calling for the removal of mercury switches from end-of-life vehicles, the law requires manufacturers to report to the state on their progress in minimizing hazardous materials and maximizing the recyclable yield of their products. "What Arkansas has done is pose a series of questions that manufacturers have to respond to annually by law that ask, 'What have we done to design our products better?'" says Reiter. According to Reiter, a similar bill was approved in North Carolina, and several other states are looking into it.

[DFR's] proponents hope that consumer pressure more than legislative pressure will play a larger role in implementing Design for Recycling in the United States.

In Europe, some of the latest European Union legislation has the same idea in mind. The End-of-Life Vehicle (ELV) Directive, which was enacted in October 2000, calls for similar and even stricter measures of recycling-friendly manufacturing of automobiles. For example, ELV-compliant cars on the market after July 1, 2003, cannot contain mercury, hexavalent chromium, lead or cadmium, with a few exceptions, according to EUROPA, the official Web site of the EU. "Globally, we are seeing a number of instances where Design for Recycling is being incorporated, at least conceptually, and that is a motivation, especially for global manufacturers," says Scott Horne, vice president of government relations and general counsel for ISRI.

However, while legislation is one way to encourage manufacturers to produce more recyclable products, Design for Recycling proponents hope to keep the initiative mostly out of the realm of legislative mandate and to make it a more voluntary practice in the United States.

Consuming Power

"We're trying to say, 'Do it voluntarily, it'll be good in the long run,'" says Horne of ISRI's Design for Recycling policy.

The initiative's proponents hope that consumer pressure more than legislative pressure will play a larger role in implementing Design for Recycling in the United States. "Manufacturers are really driven by what consumers want," says Alan Ratner, chair of ISRI's Design for Recycling Task Force and president of Metal Management Northeast. "Incentives can come legislatively, which is occurring elsewhere in the world, but the principal pressure is the buyer." Rick Gross, director of environmental affairs for the Electronics Industry Alliance (EIA), an Arlington, Va.–based trade association representing manufacturers and retailers, agrees. "The biggest single driver toward design improvement is market innovation and competition," he says. Gross says that as electronic products become more homogenized, manufacturers that can tout recyclable design can distinguish themselves in the marketplace.

Part of Design for Recycling, therefore, is public education. "We're looking at trying to introduce something in the U.S. that would cause the average buying public to want to participate and let the manufacturer know that they would prefer to buy products that are more recyclable." A labeling system could inform consumers of a product's recyclability, says Manny Bodner, ISRI Gulf Coast Chapter president and president of Bodner Metal & Iron Corp., Houston. "You don't have to tell a consumer what to buy—I sincerely believe that the consumer will make the right decision," Bodner says. "If an item is 100-percent recyclable or 90-percent recyclable, then that is going to be a very powerful incentive to induce the manufacturer to provide a product that his customer will want to purchase."

Even with willing manufacturers and an eager consuming public, DFR has challenges to face.

However, labeling could prove more applicable to some products than others. Laptop computers, for instance, already require many regulatory labels, and manufacturers might prove resistant to additional ones, says Gross. However, he says that recycled content and other Design for Recycling information could be included on the manufacturing company's Web site or in the product's owner's manual, if not on the actual product itself.

Just how much the environmentally friendly factor means to consumers is tough to judge, says Chuck Carr, vice president of communications for ISRI. "It truly depends on the consumer," he says. "But more and more today you're seeing people interested in automobiles with energy efficiency— you're getting a much more savvy consumer." Carr likens the situation to that of airbags in automobiles. "Years ago, manufacturers resisted airbags because of cost, and now they're trying to outdo themselves putting this feature in," he says. "Consumers became more educated and showed with their buying practices that cars with airbags are worth the extra cost."

However, even with willing manufacturers and an eager consuming public, DFR has challenges to face.

The Problem with Plastic

The use of plastics, especially in electronic consumer products, creates a number of hurdles for manufacturers interested in pursuing Design for Recycling. For one thing, multiple resins used in the design and manufacturing phase can complicate recycling the product at the end of its useful life.

In addition, plastics recycling is still playing catch-up in many ways to the more established practice of scrap metal recycling. In regards to recycled plastics, "there's a bias on the part of engineers, a perception that [recycled content] materials are inferior," says Horne. Use of secondary commodities in the metal and paper industry is so well established that quality is scarcely questioned on a whole, but the plastic industry is still working to overcome that manufacturing bias, he says.

That bias, in part, could be assigned to the fact that plastic polymers will degrade over time, says Gross. This results in some recycled plastic components being used in applications with less stringent quality specifications as they are recycled over and over again, from a computer casing to a car bumper and eventually as fuel stock because of its petroleum content, as an example, says Gross. This characteristic puts plastic at a distinct disadvantage when compared to scrap metal recycling. "Metal you can use as if it was new," he says.

Plastic consumer products also face problems with hazardous materials that make recycling dangerous. While vehicles have mercury switches and lead components, plastics have brominated compounds, which are often used as flame-retardants in computer casings and other consumer electronics, says Reiter. Manufacturers interested in DFR are looking for substitutes for brominated compounds, he says.

Other manufacturers try to avoid using them at all. According to Apple.com, Apple uses plastic enclosure parts that do not contain flame-retardants in several of its products to help it meet Design for Recycling standards. Some manufacturers turn to redesign to avoid the use of flame retardants altogether by constructing the product so that the power supply is farther away from the casing, according to Chris Cleet, EIA's manager of environmental affairs.

In addition to redesigning products to facilitate recycling, there has also been progress made in the industry to improve plastics recycling, says Gross, especially when it comes to separation technology. "The processes of separating are becoming better so the material is becoming purer," he says. Product assembly and disassembly is another arena where manufacturers can make products easier to recycle. "Using fewer screws, which several companies are doing, when assembling the product makes it easier and less costly to disassemble at the end of life," says Gross.

Eye on the Future

Design for Recycling proponents say that planning for recycling from a product's design stage will have broader positive effects on the environment as a whole and not just make life easier for recyclers. "There's probably nine or 10 well-recognized areas that Design for Recycling can influence our lives [in]," says Ratner. DFR can affect the environment by making products easier to recycle, decreasing the risks posed to workers by creating products that are safer to recycle and by preserving raw materials, according to Ratner.

These bigger goals are just as important, says Ratner. "Design for Recycling is a core principle to our beliefs as recyclers because it embodies so many aspects what we're trying to influence and shape in our businesses and everyday lives."

America Must Transition from Fossil Fuels to Renewable Energy

Tony Dutzik, Alexios Monopolis, Timothy Telleen-Lawton, Rob Sargent, and Anna Aurilio

Tony Dutzik is a senior policy analyst with Frontier Group, a research arm of the Vermont Public Interest Research Group. Alexios Monopolis is a writer and photographer. Timothy Telleen-Lawton is a Stanford University student. Rob Sargent is the senior energy policy analyst for the U.S. Public Interest Research Group, or USPIRG. Anna Aurilio is the legislative director of USPIRG.

A merica can and must move away from our dependence on oil and other fossil fuels and toward a New Energy Future. We can do this by tapping into our abundant supplies of clean, renewable, home-grown energy sources and by deploying our technological know-how to use energy more efficiently.

The New Energy Platform

Recognizing the promise of energy efficiency and renewable energy to transform our economy, a group of environmental, consumer, labor and civic organizations have endorsed the New Energy Future platform, which consists of the following four goals:

1. *Reduce our dependence on oil* by saving one-third of the oil we use today by 2025 (7 million barrels per day).

2. *Harness clean, renewable, home-grown energy sources* like wind, solar and farm-based biofuels for at least a quarter of all energy needs by 2025.

3. *Save energy* with high performance homes, buildings and appliances so that by 2025 we use 10 percent less energy than we do today.

4. *Invest in a New Energy Future* by committing $30 billion over the next 10 years to the New Energy for America Initiative, thus tripling research and development funding for the energy-saving and renewable energy technologies we need to achieve these goals.

In fall 2006, we released a white paper describing a plausible scenario for achieving those targets and estimating the benefits in terms of fossil fuel savings that would result. According to that analysis, America could achieve major reductions in the use of all fossil fuels by realizing the goals of the New Energy Future platform. By 2025, America could:

- Save *10.8 million barrels of oil* per day, equal to four-fifths the amount of oil we currently import from all other nations in the world.

- Save *9.1 trillion cubic feet of natural gas* per year, nearly twice as much as is currently used annually in all of America's homes and more than is currently used in all of America's industrial facilities.

- Save *900 million tons of coal per year*, or about 80 percent of all the coal we consumed in the United States in 2005.

- Save *1.7 billion megawatt-hours of electricity* per year, 30 percent more than was used in all the households in America in 2005.

Achieving these fossil fuel savings would help solve many of America's pressing energy problems—ranging from dependence on foreign oil to global warming—and would likely do so while creating jobs and contributing to the long-term stability of America's economy.

Numerous technologies exist to reduce energy use in homes and businesses.

This paper describes the technologies—many of which exist today—that can enable America to achieve the goals of the New Energy Future platform.

Energy Efficiency Technologies

Numerous technologies exist to reduce energy use in homes and businesses:

- Home weatherization—including air sealing, insulation and window replacement—can cut energy use for home heating by 20 to 30 percent.

- Efficient furnaces, like those meeting federal Energy Star standards, can cut energy use for heating by 20 percent compared to today's furnaces and by 40 percent compared to those 20 years old or older.

- Solar and heat pump water heaters can reduce energy use for water heating by half to two-thirds, and more water-efficient clothes washers and dishwashers can provide additional savings.

- Businesses can save energy, too. Wal-Mart, for example, has already committed to reducing its in-store energy use by 20 percent. And one recent analysis found that the use of more efficient motors and improved controls in the industrial, electric and commercial sectors could reduce *total* U.S. electricity demand by as much as 15 to 25 percent.

- New technologies and combinations of technologies—such as those included in zero-energy homes and low-energy commercial buildings—could lead to even more dramatic reductions in fossil fuel use in homes, business and industry in the years to come.

Oil-Saving Technologies

America can significantly reduce its consumption of oil by making cars go farther on a gallon of gasoline, reducing the rate of growth of vehicle travel, and using plant-based fuels to substitute for some of the oil we use for transportation.

- Fuel-efficient technologies like advanced engines and transmissions and improved electronics can improve the fuel economy of today's cars by 50 percent or more, while hybrid-electric and other advanced vehicles make a 45 miles per gallon [MPG] fuel economy standard feasible within the next two decades. Similar improvements can be made to the fuel economy of heavy-duty trucks.

- High gasoline prices are already reducing the growth of vehicle travel in the United States, but expanding the range of transportation choices—through expanded transit and increased support for carpooling, telecommuting, walking and biking—could enable more Americans to avoid high prices at the pump and increasingly frustrating commutes.

- Production of plant-based fuels like ethanol and biodiesel in the United States has more than doubled [from 2002 to 2006], helping to reduce our dependence on petroleum. New technologies that convert plant residues and energy crops into biofuels could make biofuels a more promising alternative and allow us to further reduce our use of oil in transportation.

- New automotive technologies—like "plug-in" hybrids—are being developed that could bring the dream of 100 MPG cars within reach, or even eliminate the use of oil in vehicles altogether.

Renewable Energy Technologies

America has access to immense renewable energy resources from the sun, earth and crops and from the movement of wind and water. The technology to tap those resources is advancing rapidly and is increasingly competitive in cost with fossil fuel technologies.

- The wind blowing through the Great Plains could generate enough electricity to power the entire country. Wind power installations in the United States have doubled [from 2002 to 2006], and wind power is among the cheapest sources of new power generation in some parts of the country.

- Solar energy could conceivably generate more than enough electricity to power the entire United States. The cost of solar panels has declined dramatically in recent years and solar power installations worldwide nearly doubled between 2002 and 2004. Continued advances in solar technology could bring solar power within reach of more Americans within the next several years.

- Plant-based sources of energy, called "biomass," already provide a substantial amount of energy in America and can provide even more. A federal advisory group has set a target of having biomass account for 5 percent of industrial and electric generator energy use by 2020.

- Immense amounts of energy are contained within the earth. Experts estimate that as much as 100,000 megawatts of geothermal power—equal to about 10 percent of today's electricity generation capacity—could be economically viable in the United States.

Federal Investments Needed

Improving today's clean energy technologies and developing tomorrow's technologies requires a substantial investment in federal energy research and development.

- Federal investment in clean energy research and development (R&D) has resulted in many technological breakthroughs with big dividends for America's economy. A study by the National Academy of Sciences estimated that R&D breakthroughs in just six energy efficiency technologies yielded economic benefits of about $30 billion on an R&D investment of about $400 million—a return on investment of 75-to-1.

- Federal investment in energy research and development has declined dramatically from its peak during the energy crises of the late 1970s and early 1980s. The United States now spends less than half as much on energy R&D programs in the public and private sectors as it did in 1980. Clean energy programs have faced continued funding pressure in recent [George W.] Bush administration budget proposals.

- Increasing federal clean energy research and development funding to $3 billion per year—about triple today's funding level—over 10 years would enable researchers to focus on several goals: improving the performance and economic competitiveness of existing clean energy technologies; redesigning our energy system to remove existing hurdles to improved energy efficiency and the integration of renewable energy into our economy; designing new energy efficiency and renewable energy technologies; reducing the cost of producing clean energy technologies and coordinating "real world" demonstration of those technologies; addressing any social or environmental impacts of clean energy technologies.

Federal Policy Changes Needed

The United States should adopt the goals of the New Energy Future platform and marshal the political, economic and scientific resources necessary to meet those goals. Public policy changes can play an important role in advancing the nation toward the goals of the New Energy Future platform. The following policies would represent a strong first step:

Energy Efficiency in Homes, Business and Industry

- Set strong energy efficiency standards for household and commercial appliances.

- Strengthen residential and commercial building codes and ensure that they are adequately enforced.

- Require utilities to meet growing energy needs through energy efficiency improvements before building new power plants.

- Expand and invest in energy efficiency programs to help homeowners and businesses install the latest technologies in their homes and businesses.

- Eliminate obstacles to the use of combined heat and power (CHP), which would dramatically improve opportunities for industrial and commercial energy efficiency.

Oil Savings

- Increase fuel economy standards for cars, light trucks and SUVs to 45 miles per gallon over the next decadeand-a-half and set strong fuel economy standards for heavy-duty trucks.

- Set goals for the use of plant-based fuels like ethanol and biodiesel and enact policies that ensure that those fuels are developed cleanly and efficiently.

- Encourage the development and use of advanced technology vehicles like "plug-in" hybrids that can achieve 100 miles per gallon of gasoline or more.

- Invest in expanded and improved public transit service, promote "smart growth" practices that reduce the need for driving, and encourage other transportation choices like telecommuting, carpooling, biking and walking.

Renewable Energy

- Enact a national renewable energy standard, similar to those already in place in 20 states, that would require a minimum percentage of the nation's electricity to come from renewable sources.

- Increase research and development funding to develop the next generation of renewable energy technologies.

- Provide consistent, long-term tax incentives for the installation of renewable energy technologies.

- Require utilities to prioritize renewable energy development over the construction of conventional power plants to satisfy electricity demand.

The World Should Not Rely on Nuclear Power to Prevent Global Warming

Rosalie Bertell and Alexey Yablakov

Rosalie Bertell is a world-renowned public health and environmental policy consultant. Alexey Yablakov is a prominent Russian environmentalist and a former adviser to former Russian president Boris Yeltsin.

So many times nuclear power has put forth its ugly head as the saviour of the world. Remember the discovery of acid rain? Nuclear power was . . . touted as the saviour technology. It was soon clear that even though nuclear power did not emit sulfuric acid or its precursors, it did emit beta particles which reacted with the nitrogen in the air causing nitric acid. In fact, the atmospheric nuclear testing may well have been the original culprit bringing about the acid rain crisis. Certainly during those years the pH of our lakes shifted toward acid, and many industrial processes and automobiles then added to the disaster.

Next, nuclear power stepped forward in the 1970's to save us from OPEC [Organization of Petroleum Exporting Countries] and high gas pricing. The crisis quickly went away, not because of nuclear power, but because the people learned to conserve energy.

Now we have nuclear power standing front and center to save us from the horrors of climate change and global warming. The thinking is again faulty, as so many have shown, but this time the "hype" and lobbying is somewhat more over-

Rosalie Bertell and Alexey Yablakov, "Nuclear Salvation: We've Heard It Before: The Nuclear Industry Will Be Emitting as Much Carbon Dioxide from Mining and Treating Its Ore as It Saves from the So-Called Clean Power It Produces," *Catholic New Times*, vol. 30, no. 1, January 15, 2006, p. 8. Copyright 2006 Catholic New Times, Inc. Reproduced by permission of the authors.

whelming. Is nuclear power really our only sane choice, or is this a last ditch stand for a failed industry?

Specious Claims for Nuclear Power

The claims for nuclear power are at best specious, at worst disastrous. Take carbon emission. There is a blithe notion that nuclear power is clean; it emits no CO_2 [carbon dioxide] and therefore does not contribute to global warming. This argument has been systematically refuted [for] years by two independent experts, Jan Willem Storm van Leeuwen and Philip Bartlett Smith. One is a chemist and energy specialist, the other a nuclear physicist, who between them have several lifetimes experience in the nuclear industry. What they have done is look at the entire life cycle of a nuclear power station, from the mining of the uranium to the storage of the resulting nuclear waste. Their conclusions make grim reading for any nuclear advocate.

The number of nuclear plants required to meet the world's needs would be colossal.

They say that at the present rate of use, worldwide supplies of rich uranium ore will soon become exhausted, perhaps within the next decade. Nuclear power stations of the future will have to rely on second-grade ore, which requires huge amounts of conventional energy to refine it. For each ton of poor-quality uranium, some 5,000 tons of granite that contain it will have to be mined, milled and then disposed of. This could rise to 10,000 tons if the quality deteriorates further. At some point, and it could happen soon, the nuclear industry will be emitting as much carbon dioxide from mining and treating its ore as it saves from the so-called clean power it produces, thanks to nuclear fission.

At this stage, according to an article in *Prospect* magazine by the energy writer David Fleming, nuclear power production would go into energy deficit. It would be putting more energy into the process than it could extract from it. Its contribution to meeting the world's energy needs would become negative! The so-called reliability of nuclear power, which its proponents enthuse over, would therefore rest on the growing use of fossil fuels rather than their replacement.

Even worse, the number of nuclear plants required to meet the world's needs would be colossal. At present, about 440 nuclear reactors supply about two percent of demand. The Massachusetts Institute of Technology calculates that 1,000 more would be needed to raise this even to 10 percent of need. At this point, the search for new sources of ore would become critical. Where would they come from? Not friendly Canada, which produces most of it at present, but places like Kazakhstan, hardly the most stable of democracies. So much for secure sources of energy! We would find ourselves out of the oil-producing frying pan, right in the middle of the ore-manufacturing fire.

The decision to go nuclear will, ironically, make the case for renewable energy stronger rather than weaker.

These arguments have to be met before other, more searching questions are answered about what the society suffers from routine emissions of radioactive materials into air and land, where we intend to store waste, what we are going to do to prevent unexpected radioactive leaks, and how we should protect nuclear plants against terrorism. The truth is that this form of energy is no more safe, reliable or clean than the others. That may well mean turning our backs on it. Some good, however, may come from the debate. The decision to go nuclear will, ironically, make the case for renewable energy stronger rather than weaker.

The Case for Renewable Energy

There are sustained local campaigns and derisive columns from the pro-nuclear lobby. They [renewable technologies] have one great advantage, however; they are genuinely renewable, and they are reversible. A wind turbine, unlike a nuclear reactor, can be removed once it has come to the end of its natural life. A wave machine can simply be towed away.

Nor, in comparison to nuclear power, are they gravely inefficient. Of course a wind farm depends on wind, which may or may not blow, and a wave machine similarly is weather-dependent. But both need to be part of the world's energy jigsaw puzzle. It is absurd, for instance, that the government is withholding the millions of dollars of investment that is needed to turn wave power into a commercial proposition. Experiments in the Orkney Islands have proved so promising that the Portuguese government has bought the technology and is hoping to exploit it industrially in its own waters. Why can't we do the same? It is only years of government subsidy which has made the nuclear option seem to be cheap!

Nuclear power generation is not trouble-free, and the more you look at it, the more enticing the other choices become.

Numerous Solutions Now Exist to Reduce Global Warming

Union of Concerned Scientists

The Union of Concerned Scientists is a nonprofit science-based advocacy organization founded in 1969 at the Massachusetts Institute of Technology.

For years we have heard so much about the causes of climate change, that we've missed the fact that there are simple, practical solutions that can slow this growing problem. Technologies exist today that can cut emissions of heat-trapping gases and make a real difference in the health of our planet. And these solutions will be good for our economy, reduce our dependence on foreign oil, and enhance our energy security.

A Challenge We Can Meet

Global warming doesn't just mean balmy February days in northern climes. It also means increasingly hot days in the summer, and a host of negative impacts that are already under way and are expected to intensify in the coming decades.

- More heat waves will likely increase the risk of heat-related illnesses and deaths.

- Cities and towns along the nation's major rivers will experience more severe and frequent flooding.

- Some areas will likely experience more extensive and prolonged droughts.

- Some of our favorite coastal and low-lying vacation areas, such as parts of the Florida Keys and Cape Cod [Massachusetts], will be much less appealing as sea levels rise, dunes erode, and the areas become more vulnerable to coastal storms.

- Many families and businesses, who have made their living from fishing, farming, and tourism could lose their livelihoods, and others who love hunting, boating, skiing, birdwatching, and just relaxing near lakes, streams, and wetlands will see some of their favorite places irretrievably changed.

The burning of fossil fuel (oil, coal, and natural gas) alone accounts for about 75 percent of annual CO_2 emissions from human activities.

The solutions to climate change are here and it's time we put them to use. If we get started today we can tackle this problem and decrease the unpleasant outcomes that await us if we do nothing. The steps we need to take are common sense. And, more often than not, they will save consumers money. The cost of inaction, however, is unacceptably high.

We Must Act Now

The scientific consensus is in. Our planet is warming, and we are helping make it happen by adding more heat-trapping gases, primarily carbon dioxide (CO_2), to the atmosphere. The burning of fossil fuel (oil, coal, and natural gas) alone accounts for about 75 percent of annual CO_2 emissions from human activities. Deforestation—the cutting and burning of forests that trap and store carbon—accounts for about another 20 percent.

Procrastination is not an option. Scientists agree that if we wait 10, 20, or 50 years, the problem will be much more difficult to address and the consequences for us will be that much more serious.

The longer we keep polluting, the longer it will take to recover and the more irreversible damage will be done.

We're treating our atmosphere like we once did our rivers. We used to dump waste thoughtlessly into our waterways, believing that they were infinite in their capacity to hold rubbish. But when entire fisheries were poisoned and rivers began to catch fire, we realized what a horrible mistake that was. Our atmosphere has limits too. CO_2 remains in the atmosphere for about 100 years. The longer we keep polluting, the longer it will take to recover and the more irreversible damage will be done. . . .

The following five sensible steps are available today and can have an enormous impact on the problem. . . .

Make Better Cars and SUVs

The technology exists to build cars, minivans, and SUVs that are just as powerful and safe as vehicles on the road today, but get 40 miles per gallon (mpg) or more. Better transmissions and engines, more aerodynamic designs, and stronger yet lighter material for chassis and bodies can cost-effectively increase the average fuel economy of today's automotive fleet from 24 mpg to 40 mpg over 10 years. This would be equivalent to taking 44 million cars off the road—and it would save individual drivers thousands of dollars in fuel costs over the life of a vehicle. Because transportation accounts for nearly 30 percent of U.S. annual CO_2 emissions, raising fuel economy is one of the most important things we can do to slow climate change.

The first step is to require Detroit [auto manufacturers] to offer consumers more fuel-efficient vehicles by raising the average gas mileage—the Corporate Average Fuel Economy (CAFE)—of their fleets. It is especially important to bring SUVs up to the same standards as cars.

More than half of America's electricity is produced from outdated, coal-burning power plants that dump pollutants and heat-trapping gases into our atmosphere.

The government can also help by offering tax credits to consumers who buy advanced technology vehicles such as today's hybrids (a combination of gasoline and self-charging electric battery engines) and new fuel cell vehicles that will hit the market within the next decade. This will give millions of people the incentive to do the right thing and help automakers create a market for clean technologies. Honda and Toyota already have highly fuel-efficient hybrid vehicles on the market that get more than 47 mpg. . . .

Modernize America's Electricity System

More than half of America's electricity is produced from outdated, coal-burning power plants that dump pollutants and heat-trapping gases into our atmosphere. In fact, power plants are the single largest source of CO_2—one-third of the U.S. total. However, cost effective, clean energy sources do exist. By increasing our use of clean renewable energy, investing in energy efficiency, and reducing pollution from fossil fuel plants we can save money for consumers, reduce heat-trapping emissions, and lessen the need for new coal or gas power plants.

A study by the Union of Concerned Scientists [UCS] found that we could reduce power plant CO_2 emissions by 60 percent compared with government forecasts for 2020. Consumers would save a total of $440 billion—reaching $350 annually per family by 2020.

A national standard requiring 10 percent of our electricity to be generated from renewable energy sources by 2020 is an attainable goal. We are already using clean, safe, renewable sources such as solar, wind, geothermal, and biomass (fuel from plant matter) to produce clean energy. Costs for these technologies have dropped dramatically since they were first introduced decades ago. For instance, the cost of wind energy has decreased from 40 cents per kilowatt hour in 1980 to between three cents and six cents today.

Twenty states have already adopted standards requiring utilities to offer more renewable energy to consumers.

We can reduce our emissions of heat-trapping gases by establishing a Renewable Electricity Standard that requires utilities to generate 10 percent of our power from clean renewable energy sources like wind, solar, and bioenergy. UCS and EIA [Energy Information Administration] analysis of a 10 percent standard show that carbon dioxide emissions would be reduced 166 million to 215 million metric tons nationally by 2020, equivalent to taking 32 million cars off the road. In addition to curbing global warming, increasing our reliance on homegrown renewable energy would also grow our economy. According to a UCS study, *Renewing America's Economy*, the 10 percent standard would save consumers $28.2 billion by 2020, create more than 190,000 jobs, and provide $41.5 billion in new capital investment.

Twenty states have already adopted standards requiring utilities to offer more renewable energy to consumers. Texas, the heart of the nation's fossil fuel industry, has one of the biggest, most successful markets for new renewable energy plants in the United States. In fact the Renewable Portfolio Standard in Texas has been so successful that in July 2005, the Texas Legislature voted to increase it. If Texas can do it, so can the rest of the nation.

To be most effective, a national renewable standard should be implemented in concert with measures to reduce the pollution coming from coal, oil, and gas power plants. The current mix of pollutants pouring out from power plants causes smog, acid rain, and mercury poisoning as well as global warming. Addressing all four major pollutants (sulfur dioxide, nitrogen oxides, mercury, and CO_2) at once allows utilities to take an integrated approach to pollution control, reducing industry costs and greatly increasing the public health benefits. . . .

Increase Energy Efficiency in Homes and Businesses

Like better technology for transportation and power generation, the technology for more efficient motors, appliances, windows, homes, and manufacturing processes is here today. These simple solutions save consumers money and can have an enormous impact on climate change at the same time. For instance, in the past two decades, energy-efficiency standards for household appliances kept 53 million tons of heat-trapping gases out of the air each year.

New or updated standards are now in place for many major appliances, including clothes washers, dishwashers, water heaters, furnaces, and boilers. In 2006, new standards for air conditioners take effect that will increase efficiency 23 percent compared with the current standard. By 2020, these efficiency gains alone will reduce the need for up to 150 new medium-sized (300 megawatt) power plants. Efficiency standards for commercial equipment such as refrigerators, heaters, furnaces, and public lighting also have significant room for improvement.

Many states and utilities have energy efficiency programs. They typically save consumers more than $2 in lower energy bills for every $1 invested in efficiency. A federal matching fund created by a $1 per household surcharge on monthly electric bills could provide more than $7 billion per year in funding for state energy efficiency and renewable energy programs. . . .

We invest far more in [government] subsidies for the fossil fuel and nuclear industries today than on R&D for renewable energy or advanced vehicle technologies.

Protect Threatened Forests

In addition to sheltering more than half of the planet's species and providing benefits such as clean drinking water, forests play a critical role in climate change: they store carbon, the base of CO_2. When forests are burned, cleared, or otherwise degraded, their stored carbon is released into the atmosphere. Tropical deforestation now accounts for about 20 percent of all human-caused CO_2 emissions each year.

Here in the United States, we should manage our forests in a way that helps our climate. For instance, the forests of the Pacific Northwest and Southeast could double their storage of carbon if timber managers lengthened the time between harvests and allowed older trees to remain standing. Looking beyond our borders, we should develop partnerships with developing countries to help them better conserve their forests. We should also set up a system that allows private companies to get credit for reducing carbon when they acquire and permanently set aside natural forests for conservation. . . .

Support American Ingenuity

The Manhattan Project. The Apollo Program. The silicon chip. The Internet. Time and again, America has proven that putting together the best minds and the right resources can result in technological breakthroughs that change the course of human history.

Federal research money has already played an integral part in our progress in developing renewable energy sources and improving energy efficiency. In the past 20 years, the Department of Energy's efficiency initiatives have saved the country 5.5 quadrillion BTUs [British thermal units] of energy and nearly $30 billion in avoided energy costs. Federal research dollars have driven technological advances in fuel cells. This technology, which runs engines on hydrogen fuel and emits only water vapor, is key to moving our transportation system away from the polluting combustion engine and freeing the United States from its oil dependence.

Vigorous support for research and development [R&D] is critical to achieving practical solutions. Yet, we invest far more in subsidies for the fossil fuel and nuclear industries today than on R&D for renewable energy or advanced vehicle technologies. For instance, Congress appropriated $736 million for fossil fuel research and $667 million for nuclear research in 2001, but only $376 million for all renewable energy technologies combined. The President's Committee of Advisors on Science and Technology recommended we double spending on energy efficiency and renewable energy technologies. This is a good start. Vehicle research should also be increased and refocused on technologies and fuels that can deliver the greatest environmental gains, including hybrid and fuel cell cars, renewable ethanol fuel, and the cleanest forms of hydrogen production.

In addition, we should continue to study storing carbon underground (geologic carbon sequestration) as a potentially viable way to reduce CO_2 released into the atmosphere. CO_2 could be captured at the power plant or other production unit and returned underground. While this technology holds some promise, it is still under development and its environmental impacts must be fully explored before it is widely implemented.

International Cooperation Is Necessary to Affect Global Warming

Melissa Gorelick

Melissa Gorelick is a contributing writer for UN Chronicle, *a quarterly magazine published by the United Nations.*

For decades, the battle lines over oil, the world markets and the environment have been clearly drawn. But recently there has been an unprecedented shift in the conversation surrounding energy issues. Scientists and politicians have finally managed to rouse an undecided public to a climate crisis that may be "inconvenient", but is increasingly and disturbingly "true". Meanwhile, economists worldwide are attempting to dispel apocalyptic predictions about the global oil supply. The international community finds itself in the difficult position of gauging energy truths on a daily basis. How would a polar ice cap melt affect the subarctic world? What do exorbitant gas prices really mean? While oil talk is messy, its bottom line is clear: today's energy problems are global ones and require global solutions. . . .

UN Efforts

The United Nations has led the way in coordinating a unified international energy effort. Moreover, it has taken innovative steps to draw human voices into a debate that, for all its urgency, can seem daunting and inaccessible to those that it affects most: consumers and workers the world over.

Three UN treaty bodies met in May 2006 to address the economic and environmental impact of energy usage. The

Melissa Gorelick, "Oil Matters: Economic and Environmental Prospects Hinge on Global Cooperation," *UN Chronicle*, vol. 43, no. 2, July-August 2006, pp. 75–77. Copyright © 2006 United Nations. Reprinted with the permission of the United Nations.

fourteenth session of the UN Commission on Sustainable Development heard from groups as varied as trade union leaders, indigenous representatives and technology specialists as it discussed a long-term international energy strategy. A week later, the UN Permanent Forum on Indigenous Issues held a regional meeting on the Arctic, where representatives of the Arctic Council spoke passionately about the changes occurring in their homelands. Finally, the UN Framework Convention on Climate Change (UNFCCC) met in Bonn, Germany, during the 24th session of subsidiary bodies to tackle the issue of a post–Kyoto Protocol strategy for the first time. The Protocol's initial commitment period, ratified by 163 States in an attempt to lower global energy emissions, expires in 2012.

In everyday economic terms, a strong case exists for curbing fuel usage . . . across the planet.

Divisions Between Countries

Keeping fossil fuels available, realistically priced and environmentally friendly goes beyond what Governments alone are able to do. However, energy debates have nonetheless been plagued by regional strife, and cooperation is often elusive. The question of energy-specific regulations has been a contentious one for countries with high or rapidly rising industry levels, such as the United States, China and India. In 2001, the United States formally withdrew from the Protocol, citing the need for more country-specific guidelines. China has likewise refused to sign, worrying that the treaty does not take into account its energy needs as a rapidly developing nation and asserting that as the world's most populated State its emissions should be measured per capita. Both China and India contend that they will persist in requiring substantial energy supplies as they continue to develop.

Leading UN environmental bodies like the UNFCCC acknowledge that such divisions between industrialized and developing countries are a problem. Working under the principle of industrialized response, the Kyoto Protocol and other environmental agreements urge that industrialized nations lead the way in emissions reduction, while developing nations have only semi-voluntary participation standards. UNFCCC, however, has seen the conflict as an opportunity to launch radically progressive environmental and economic programmes, according to Hennig Wuester, Special Assistant to the UNFCCC Executive Secretary.

The Clean Development Mechanism (CDM) of the Protocol, for example, offers industrialized nations the chance to invest in the energy clean-up of developing nations and use this as credit towards their own emissions targets. Such projects create a cohesive global goal from what was once a series of detached regional problems. Indications are that these unifying incentives are working, said Mr. Wuester. The UNFCCC Secretariat estimates that CDM will reduce worldwide emissions by over 1 billion tonnes [1.1 billion U.S. tons] by the end of 2012—a success that will prove to be a great promoter of international cooperation. "It's a sign that the institutional set-up that's in place is quite powerful", he said, adding that Kyoto's critics will be hard-pressed to argue against such a vast statistic.

A Limited Amount of Oil

But in everyday economic terms, a strong case exists for curbing fuel usage even more deeply across the planet. Desmond Lachman, a fellow at the American Enterprise Institute for Public Policy, explained that short-sighted energy strategies in parts of the developing world leave the entire global economy vulnerable to price hikes. To promote industry, some Governments "suppress" oil prices by keeping domestic gas prices artificially low, even when the international price rises, he said. Encouraged by low prices, the industry and consumers in developing countries consume oil liberally, but the rest of the global community must account for this suppression by picking up the slack in oil costs, Mr. Lachman added. Combined with concerns about the political stability of the world's big oil producers, the results are drastic hikes in prices and the common, though not entirely well-founded, concern that we are scraping the bottom of the proverbial barrel.

"There is no question that you're dealing with a limited amount of oil", admitted Mr. Lachman, who echoed, however, much of the media's recent discussion that there's "little chance that we'll run out soon". George Kowalski, Executive Director of the UN Economic Commission for Europe (ECE), agreed. The Commission estimates that at today's prices and with current technology, conventional oil reserves could meet the cumulative global demand for the next forty years. A more urgent question, he said, is how to get to the estimated 65 to 75 percent of the world's hydrocarbon reserves that are out of reach of producers and distributors. These more unconventional sources of oil—such as shale and coal, both of which must be specially mined and converted into oil—require financial investments for several years before they can turn a profit. And because politics and business have already led to such a tight fuel market, many countries are unwilling to make these long-term investments.

More urgent ... than the economic frenzy surrounding oil are the environmental effects of this much desired, but increasingly scarce, fossil fuel.

Another option for cleaner, more cost-effective fuel—and one that also requires significant research investments—is the much discussed biofuels, which are viable ethanol created from products like corn or sugar cane. A recent report by the Worldwatch Institute revealed that biofuel production has doubled since 2001. Although oil still accounts for over 96 percent of fuel used in transportation worldwide, countries like Brazil—with 40 percent of its transportation already running on sugar-cane biofuel—and the United States have begun investing heavily in cleaner energy solutions. However, looking forward to the development of such radical energy sources and to alternative oil supplies, Mr. Lachman said that international standards would make sense. More nations need to invest more capital in these areas because, despite the concerns of individual nations and regions, the energy economy is fundamentally a global issue. "I think there is a clear case here for international coordination", he said. The UN multilateral framework could be a positive model for cooperative international ventures in the future.

Global Consequences of Climate Change

More urgent, perhaps, than the economic frenzy surrounding oil are the environmental effects of this much desired, but increasingly scarce, fossil fuel. Wasteful, unchecked consumption by industry and consumers, especially due to suppressed oil prices, is the leading cause of climate change—a process that threatens the very basic foundation of our environment. Over time, energy emissions, now almost universally acknowledged to be warming the planet, threaten to alter global weather patterns beyond recognition. Droughts, crop failures and famines could follow as continents struggle to adjust.

While these images are dire predictions for most, some communities are already dealing with the reality of climate change. Sheila Watt-Cloutier, Chair of the Inuit Circumpolar Conference and Special Rapporteur at the UN regional meeting on the Arctic, shared her people's experience of losing natural resources on which they have always relied. Their hardships are not isolated. Representatives of northern peoples from seven nations and several indigenous groups echoed her concerns. The Arctic Council reported success in past environmental efforts, including proactive clean-up solutions, that have begun to teach northern villages to monitor, test and contain pollution in their own backyards. However, the melting caused by greenhouse gas emissions, it said, is too big a problem to be handled locally. Ms. Watt-Cloutier stressed the need for all nations to make sacrifices in order to lower emissions even beyond the demands of the Kyoto Protocol. Without deep and coordinated reductions, she warned, the subarctic world will likely feel the effects of global warming as well. "The Arctic is the mercury in the global environmental barometer", she said. "Climate change has worldwide consequences."

Economics and the environment are integrally connected at the juncture of oil.

Through solutions like CDM, the UNFCCC parties are already tackling Artic hardships and hope to stave off further climate change. At the Bonn meeting, members continued to monitor cuts in greenhouse gas emissions and launched new initiatives, such as the "Dialogue on Long-Term Cooperative Action", a project designed to adapt the world to climate change through innovative technology and open-door international participation. An agenda for specific talks has been set, beginning in November 2006 in Nairobi, Kenya.

Economics and the environment are integrally connected at the juncture of oil. With so many varied interests at stake, the topic can be complex and daunting, but it is also a chance for meaningful international participation. This should not be forgotten as the issue continues to take on a wider global significance. Future cooperation on energy's economic front is sure to reflect environmental concerns, especially as UN leaders continue to promote the two perspectives as twin challenges to be faced.

Organizations to Contact

The editors have compiled the following list of organizations concerned with the issues debated in this book. The descriptions are derived from materials provided by the organizations. All have publications or information available for interested readers. The list was compiled on the date of publication of the present volume; the information provided here may change. Be aware that many organizations take several weeks or longer to respond to inquiries, so allow as much time as possible.

American Council for an Energy-Efficient Economy (ACEEE)
1001 Connecticut Ave., NW Suite 801
Washington, DC   20036
(202) 429-8873 • fax: (202) 429-2248
e-mail: info@aceee.org
Web site: www.aceee.org

The ACEEE is a nonprofit organization dedicated to advancing energy efficiency as a means of promoting both economic prosperity and environmental protection. ACEEE's Web site contains policy reports, press releases, testimony, and fact sheets on various energy-related issues.

American Council on Science and Health (ACSH)
1995 Broadway, 2nd Floor, New York, NY   10023-5860
(212) 362-7044 • fax: (212) 362-4919
e-mail: acsh@acsh.org
Web site: www.acsh.org

ACSH is a consumer education consortium concerned with, among other topics, issues related to the environment and health. The council publishes editorials, position papers, and books, including, for example, "Regulating Mercury Emissions from Power Plants: Will It Protect Our Health?" and "Biomonitoring: Measuring Levels of Chemicals in People—and What the Results Mean," which are available on its Web site.

American Lung Association (ALA)
61 Broadway, 6th Floor, New York, NY   10006
(212) 315-8700
Web site: www.lungusa.org

Founded in 1904 to fight tuberculosis, the ALA currently fights lung disease in all its forms, with special emphasis on asthma, tobacco control, and environmental health. Under the Air Quality link on its Web site, the ALA provides articles, fact sheets, and special reports on pollution-related issues, including its yearly "State of the Air" report.

Bluewater Network
311 California St., Suite 510, San Francisco, CA   94104
(415) 544-0790 • fax: (415) 544-0796
e-mail: bluewater@bluewaternetwork.org
Web site: www.bluewaternetwork.org

The Bluewater Network promotes policy changes in government and industry to reduce dependence on fossil fuels and eradicate other root causes of air and water pollution, global warming, and habitat destruction. On its Web site the group provides fact sheets, articles, and news on specific water pollution issues such as ship emissions, oil spills, and global warming. Articles that are available on the Web site include, for example, "Cruise Pollution Update: More Cruise Ships, More Passengers, More Pollution."

Cato Institute
1000 Massachusetts Ave. NW, Washington, DC   20001-5403
(202) 842-0200 • fax: (202) 842-3490
e-mail: cato@cato.org
Web site: www.cato.org

The Cato Institute is a libertarian public policy research foundation dedicated to limiting the role of government and protecting individual liberties. The institute publishes the quarterly magazine *Regulation*, and the bimonthly *Cato Policy*

Report. Its Web site contains a research topic called "Environment and Climate" that provides links to a wealth of Cato publications dealing with pollution, the environment, and global warming.

Clear the Air

1200 Eighteenth St. NW, 5th Floor, Washington, DC   20036
(202) 887-1715 • fax: (202) 887-8877
e-mail: info@cleartheair.org
Web site: www.cleartheair.org

Clear the Air, which supports stricter air pollution controls, is a joint project of three leading clean air groups: the Clean Air Task Force, the National Environmental Trust, and the U.S. Public Interest Research Group (USPIRG) Education Fund. On its Web site Clear the Air publishes news releases, fact sheets, and reports, including "Premature Deaths from New Coal-Fired Power Plants in Texas," "Season Creep: How Global Warming Is Already Affecting the World Around Us," and "Water in the West."

Competitive Enterprise Institute (CEI)

1001 Connecticut Ave. NW, Suite 1250
Washington, DC   20036
(202) 331-1010 • fax: (202) 331-0640
e-mail: info@cei.org
Web site: www.cei.org

CEI is a public policy organization dedicated to the principles of free enterprise and limited government. The institute supports market-based pollution policies. On its Web site CEI publishes books, articles, editorials, speeches, and studies, including "Biofuels, Food, or Wildlife? The Massive Land Costs of U.S. Ethanol" and "The Responsible Corporation."

Earth Island Institute

300 Broadway, Suite 28, San Francisco, CA   94133-3312
(415) 788-3666 • fax: (415) 788-7324
Web site: www.earthisland.org

Founded in 1982 by veteran environmentalist David Brower, Earth Island promotes the conservation, preservation, and restoration of Earth. The institute publishes the quarterly *Earth Island Journal*, and recent articles include "An Inconvenient Truth and Who Killed the Electric Car" and "The Battered Border: Immigration Policy Sacrifices Arizona Wilderness."

Earth Policy Institute
1350 Connecticut Ave. NW, Suite 403
Washington, DC   20036
(202) 496-9290 • fax: (202) 496-9325
e-mail: epi@earthpolicy.org
Web site: www.earth-policy.org

The Earth Policy Institute is an organization dedicated to providing a vision of an environmentally sustainable economy, or eco-economy. Its Web site provides links to various publications, including "Eco-Economy Updates" and reports such as "A New Materials Economy" and "2005 Another Record Year for Global Carbon Emissions."

Environmental Protection Agency (EPA)
Ariel Rios Bldg., 1200 Pennsylvania Ave. NW
Washington, DC   20460
(Various phone numbers organized by topic are listed on Web site.)
Web site: www.epa.gov

The EPA is the federal agency in charge of protecting the environment and controlling pollution. The agency works toward these goals by assisting businesses and local environmental agencies, enacting and enforcing regulations, identifying and fining polluters, and cleaning up polluted sites. On its Web site EPA has links to specific pollution issues, including acid rain, the Clean Air Act, Clean Water Act, hazardous waste, Superfund, and recycling. These links include articles, memos, and speeches on a wide variety of pollution-related topics.

Friends of the Earth International
PO Box 19199, 1000 gd, Amsterdam
  The Netherlands
31 20 622 1369 • fax: 31 20 639 2181
e-mail: foe@foe.org
Web site: www.foei.org

Friends of the Earth is an international advocacy organization dedicated to protecting the planet from environmental degradation; preserving biological, cultural, and ethnic diversity; and empowering citizens to have an influential voice in decisions affecting the quality of their environment. It has a U.S. chapter and publishes numerous publications dealing with the environment. Recent publications include "How the World Bank's Energy Framework Sells the Climate and Poor People Short" and "The Tyranny of Free Trade."

GrassRoots Recycling Network (GRRN)
PO Box 282, Cotati, CA 94931
(707) 321-7883 • Web site: www.grrn.org

GRRN's mission is to eliminate the waste of natural and human resources. The network advocates corporate accountability and public policies that eliminate waste and build sustainable communities. The GRRN Web site contains information about recycling policy, practices, and future directions, together with links to articles from various sources.

Greenpeace
702 H St. NW, Washington, DC 20001
(202) 462-1177
e-mail: info@wdc.greenpeace.org

Greenpeace is a private membership organization of environmental activists with offices in more than forty countries. It stages peaceful protests and other activities to call the world's attention to environmental threats such as nuclear testing, commercial whaling, and the warming of Anarctica, and to protect the world's ancient forests and oceans. The group publishes annual reports on the state of the environment; these are available on its Web site.

The Heritage Foundation
214 Massachusetts Ave. NE, Washington, DC   20002-4999
(800) 546-4400 • fax: (202) 546-8328
e-mail: info@heritage.org
Web site: www.heritage.org

The Heritage Foundation is a conservative think tank that supports free enterprise and limited government. Its researchers criticize Environmental Protection Agency overregulation and believe that recycling is an ineffective method of dealing with waste. Its publications, such as its Backgrounder series of papers, include studies on the uncertainty of global warming and the greenhouse effect. Available on the foundation's Web site are articles such as "Warming Up to the Truth: The Real Story About Climate Change," "A Great G8, If the World Ditches Kyoto," and "Why the Government's CAFE Standards for Fuel Efficiency Should Be Repealed, Not Increased."

International Dark-Sky Association (IDA)
3225 N. First Ave., Tucson, AZ   85719-2103
(520) 293 3198 • fax: (520) 293-3192
e-mail: ida@darksky.org
Web site: www.darksky.org

IDA's goals are to reverse the adverse environmental impact on dark skies by building awareness of the problem of light pollution and the solutions, including quality nighttime lighting. On its Web site IDA publishes fact sheets, slide shows demonstrating the impact of light pollution, and articles, including "Light Pollution: The Neglected Problem."

Natural Resources Defense Council (NRDC)
40 W. Twentieth St., New York, NY   10011
(212) 727-2700
e-mail: proinfo@nrdc.org
Web site: www.nrdc.org

The NRDC is a nonprofit organization that uses law, science, and more than four hundred thousand members nationwide to protect the planet's wildlife and wild places and to ensure a safe and healthy environment for all living things. NRDC publishes *Nature's Voice*, a bimonthly bulletin of environmental news, and *OnEarth*, an environmental magazine. Its Web site also provides information about specific pollution-related topics such as clean air and energy, global warming, clean water and oceans, and toxic chemicals and health. These links include fact sheets, reports, news, and articles, including "Western Parks Endangered by Climate Disruption" and "Nuclear Power Isn't the Solution."

Physicians for Social Responsibility (PSR)
1875 Connecticut Ave. NW, Suite 1012
Washington, DC   20009
(202) 667-4260 • fax: (202) 667-4201
e-mail: psrnatl@psr.org
Web site: www.psr.org

Founded in 1961, PSR documented the presence of strontium-90—a highly radioactive waste product of atmospheric nuclear testing—in American children's teeth. This finding led rapidly to the Limited Nuclear Test Ban Treaty that ended aboveground explosions by the superpowers. PSR's mission is to address public health threats that affect people in the United States and around the world. The PSR Web site publishes fact sheets and article excerpts, including "Asthma and the Role of Air Pollution" and "Fighting Global Warming, Ending Our Dependence on Oil."

Political Economy Research Center (PERC)
2048 Analysis Dr., Suite A, Bozeman, MT   59718
(406) 587-9591
e-mail: perc@perc.org
Web site: www.perc.org

PERC is a nonprofit research and educational organization that seeks market-oriented solutions to environmental problems. Areas of research covered in the PERC Policy Series papers include endangered species, forestry, fisheries, mines, parks, public lands, property rights, hazardous waste, pollution, water, and wildlife. PERC conducts a variety of conferences, offers internships and fellowships, and provides environmental education materials. On its Web site PERC provides access to recent and archived articles, reports, and its policy series, including such titles as "Markets and Morality" and "Saving Fisheries with Free Markets."

Sierra Club
85 Second St., 2nd Floor, San Francisco, CA   94105
(415) 977-5500 • fax: (415) 977-5799
e-mail: information@sierraclub.org
Web site: www.sierraclub.org

The Sierra Club is a grassroots environmental organization with more than 750,000 members. It seeks to protect and restore the natural and human environment and promote the responsible use of Earth's resources. It publishes *Sierra* magazine and a newsletter called *Sierra Club Insider*. The group's Web site also contains links to numerous books published by the group, including, for example, *The Case Against the Global Economy* and *In the Absence of the Sacred*.

Union of Concerned Scientists (UCS)
2 Brattle Sq., Cambridge, MA   02238-9105
(617) 547-5552 • fax: (617) 864-9405
Web site: www.ucsusa.org

The UCS is a science-based nonprofit advocacy group that works for a healthy environment and a safer world. UCS publishes a semiannual magazine, *Catalyst*, as well as a quarterly newsletter, *Earthwise*, a monthly list of environmental tips called *Green Tips*, and a variety of books and reports. Its Web site also contains valuable information about global warming and other environmental topics.

Worldwatch Institute
1776 Massachusetts Ave. NW, Washington, DC   20036-1904
(202) 452-1999 • fax: (202) 296-7365
e-mail: worldwatch@worldwatch.org

Web site: www.worldwatch.org

Worldwatch is a nonprofit public policy research organization dedicated to informing policy makers and the public about emerging global problems and trends and the complex links between the world economy and its environmental support systems. It publishes the bimonthly *World Watch* magazine, the Environmental Alert series, and several policy papers. Recent and archived issues of *World Watch* are available on its Web site.

Bibliography

Books

Richard N.L. Andrews	*Managing the Environment, Managing Ourselves: A History of American Environmental Policy*, 2nd ed. New Haven, CT: Yale University Press, 2006.
Harvey Blatt	*America's Environmental Report Card: Are We Making the Grade?* Cambridge, MA: MIT Press, 2005.
Paul Brown	*Global Pollution.* Chicago: Raintree, 2003.
Paul Brown	*Global Warning: The Last Chance for Change.* London: A & C Black/ Guardian Books, 2006.
Marla Cone	*Silent Snow: The Slow Poisoning of the Arctic.* New York: Grove, 2005.
Christopher D. Cook	*Diet for a Dead Planet: How the Food Industry Is Killing Us.* New York: New Press, 2004.
Devra Lee Davis	*When Smoke Ran Like Water: Tales of Environmental Deception and the Battle Against Pollution.* New York: Basic Books, 2002.
Kelly Sims Gallagher	*China Shifts Gears: Automakers, Oil, Pollution, and Development.* Cambridge, MA: MIT Press, 2006.

Roy A. Gallant	*Water: Our Precious Resource.* New York: Benchmark, 2003.
Clive Gifford	*Pollution.* Chicago: Heinemann Library, 2006.
Albert Gore	*An Inconvenient Truth: The Planetary Emergency of Global Warming and What We Can Do About It.* Emmaus, PA: Rodale, 2006.
Roy M. Harrison, ed.	*Pollution: Causes, Effects, and Control,* 4th ed. Cambridge, UK: Royal Society of Chemistry, 2001.
Marquita K. Hill	*Understanding Environmental Pollution: A Primer,* 2nd ed. New York: Cambridge University Press, 2004.
Bruce E. Johansen	*Global Warming in the 21st Century.* Westport, CT: Praeger, 2006.
Elizabeth Kolbert	*Field Notes from a Catastrophe: Man, Nature, and Climate Change.* New York: Bloomsbury, 2006.
Bjørn Lomborg	*The Skeptical Environmentalist: Measuring the Real State of the World,* New York: Cambridge University Press, 2001.
Ramón López and Michael A. Toman, eds.	*Economic Development and Environmental Sustainability: New Policy Options.* New York: Oxford University Press, 2006.
Paul McCaffrey, ed.	*Global Climate Change.* Bronx, NY: H.W. Wilson, 2006.

Robert A. Ristinen and Jack J. Kraushaar — *Energy and the Environment*, 2nd ed. Hoboken, NJ: John Wiley, 2006.

Vandana Shiva — *Water Wars: Privatization, Pollution and Profit.* Cambridge, MA: South End, 2002.

Carl J. Sindermann — *Coastal Pollution: Effects on Living Resources and Humans.* Boca Raton, FL: CRC/Taylor & Francis, 2006.

S. Fred Singer and Dennis T. Avery — *Unstoppable Global Warming: Every 1,500 Years.* Lanham, MD: Rowman & Littlefield, 2007.

James Gustave Speth — *Red Sky at Morning: America and the Crisis of the Global Environment.* New Haven, CT: Yale University Press, 2004.

Richard Stapleton, ed. — *Pollution A to Z.* New York: Macmillan Reference USA, 2004.

Mike Tidwell — *The Ravaging Tide: Strange Weather, Future Katrinas, and the Coming Death of America's Coastal Cities.* New York: Free Press, 2006.

Thomas H. Tietenberg — *Emissions Trading: Principles and Practice*, 2nd ed. Washington, DC: Resources for the Future, 2006.

B.C. Wolverton and John D. Wolverton — *Growing Clean Water: Nature's Solution to Water Pollution.* Picayune, MS: WES, 2001.

Periodicals

Adam Aston and Burt Helm | "The Race Against Climate Change: How Top Companies Are Reducing Emissions of CO2 and Other Greenhouse Gases," *Business Week*, December 12, 2005.

Felicity Barringer | "California, Taking Big Gamble, Tries to Curb Greenhouse Gases," *New York Times*, September 15, 2006. www.nytimes.com/2006/09/15/us/ 15energy.html?ex=1315972800&en=d2 aace071a8150 1c&ei=5088&partner =rssnyt&emc=rss.

Hannah Beech | "They Export Pollution Too," *Time*, June 19, 2005. http://www.time.com/ time/magazine/article/0,9171,107411 9,00.html.

Ronald S. Borod | "Greening the Planet: There Is a Payoff in Marketing Emissions in an International Marketplace," *Energy*, Spring 2006.

Business Week | "Stealing a March on the EPA," July 12, 2004.

John Carey | "Coal: Could Be the End of the Line; Prices Would Soar If the U.S. Clamped down on Carbon Emissions," *Business Week*, November 13, 2006.

Economist | "The Dirty Sky: Aircraft Emissions," June 10, 2006.

Geographical   "Averting the Disaster: With Kyoto Virtually Dead and Buried, a New Coalition of Governments Has Recently Begun to Focus on Technological Solutions. But Will They Be Enough?" December 2005.

Marc Gunther   "Supreme Court Tackles Global Warming," *Fortune*, October 27, 2006. http://money.cnn.com/2006/10/25/ news/economy/pluggedin_gunther _epa.fortune/.

Jane Lloyd   "The Link Between Environment and Disease," *UN Chronicle*, March–May 2006.

Steve Lohr   "The Energy Challenge: The Cost of an Overheated Planet," *New York Times*, December 12, 2006. www.nytimes.com/2006/12/12/ business/worldbusiness/12warm. html?n=Top%2fNews%2fScience% 2fTopics%2fGlobal%20Warming&_r =1&adxnnl=1&oref=slogin&adxnnlx =1166551415-Ufc3dfkN136406 CLOiqn2A.

Richard J. Newman   "Pollution Politics," *U.S. News & World Report*, December 27, 2004.

Newsweek   "Designing the Future: No Waste or Pollution," May 16, 2006. www.msnbc.msn.com/id/7773650/ site/newsweek/.

Newsweek International

"Force of Nature: Environmentalism Is No Longer the Province of the Left. Conservative Politicians and Big Business Have Both Jumped on the Bandwagon," August 14, 2006.

William H. Rauckhorst

"Energy Ethics: In an Era of Global Warming and Peak Oil Consumption," *America*, November 6, 2006.

Gretel H. Schueller

"Wasting Away: Is Recycling on the Skids?" *OnEarth*, Fall 2002. www.nrdc.org/onearth/02fal/recycling1.asp?r=n.

Space Daily

"Global Warming and Your Health," October 24, 2006.

Space Daily

"Global Warming Could Halt Ocean Circulation with Harmful Results," December 8, 2005.

Space Daily

"Global Warming Increases Species Extinctions Worldwide," November 15, 2006.

Space Daily

"Global Warming Producing 150,000 Deaths Annually: WHO," November 17, 2005.

Space Daily

"NASA and NOAA Announce Ozone Hole Is a Double Record Breaker," October 20, 2006.

Space Daily

"Space Sunshade Might Be Feasible in Global Warming Emergency," November 8, 2006.

Tim Worstall   "Water World: Researchers Have
                Found That the Private Sector Is Bet-
                ter than Government Entities at Pro-
                viding a Better Quality of Water,"
                Saturday Evening Post, September/
                October 2006.

Index